Scene from the life of Pius II, Siena   *Native American*   *The Empire State Building, New York*

Mayan procession   *Atomic bomb mushroom cloud*

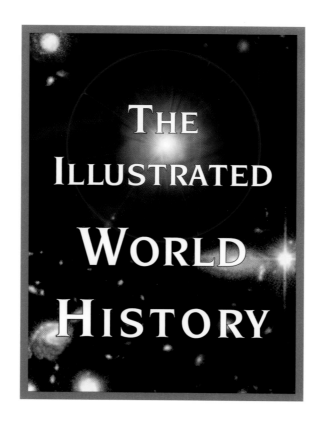

THE
ILLUSTRATED
WORLD
HISTORY

A CHRONICLE FROM THE BEGINNING OF TIME

TO THE START OF THE NEW MILLENNIUM

KEY

THE AMERICAS
EUROPE
EASTERN EUROPE AND MIDDLE EAST
INDIA
ASIA
CHINA
AFRICA
AUSTRALASIA
EXPLORERS AND TRADERS
SCIENTISTS AND INVENTORS
THE ARTS AND RELIGION
FIRST DATES

Design and illustration
Christos Kondeatis

Text contributors
Gill Davies, Jackie Fortey, Christos Kondeatis, Christine O'Brien and Caroline Thomas

Additional illustration
Paul Wright, Patrick Wright and Clive Prichard

Computer generated illustration and page make-up
Nicholas Halliday 0181-949 5077

General Editors
Jackie Fortey, Geraldine Carter and Del Tucker

Consulting Editors to Timeline
Brian AC Keaney, Winifred and Herbert Rindl

Published in 1999 by
Christos Kondeatis Designs Ltd
27 Upper Tooting Park
Upper Tooting
London SW17 7SN
Tel: 0181-672 3235 Fax: 0181-767 0595

Copyright © Christos Kondeatis 1999

ISBN 1 901582 01 9

Printed and bound in China

PHOTO CREDITS

FRONT COVER: *centre panel*; NASA (computer-generated montage of Big Bang, and galaxies in deep space). *Centre right*; Popperfoto/Reuter (Dolly the first genetically copied sheep). *Below: left*; NASA (Aldrin on the Moon), *centre*; Rex Features (Robin, Clinton & Arafat), *right*; Rex Features (Russian Coup,1991)

BACK COVER: *top left*; Photograph by Tim Graham, (Princess Diana in Korea), *top centre*; Rex Features (The Berlin Wall, 1989), *bottom right*; Courtesy of British Aerospace Military Aircraft (Harrier GR7).

INSIDE FRONT COVER: *right-hand page; top left*; Scala. *top centre*; Corbis-Bettmann, *top right*; Power Stock/Tony Wright, *below left*; E.T. Archive, *below right*; Popperfoto.

PAGES ONE TO FORTY: Courtesy of NASA: 1 (montage), 3, 4 (*top*, montage), 5, 32 *right*, 38 *below right*. John Reader/Science Photo Library: 6, 11, *sculls on top panels* 2, 3, 4, 6, 7. The Natural History Museum, London: 11, *skull on top panels* 5, 11.

Sheridan/Ancient Art & Architecture Collection: 16 *top*. E.T.Archive: 16 *below*, 21 *below*, 32 *left*, Scala: 17 *top left*, 22 *centre*, 23 *centre*, 23 *centre right*, Ecole Nationale Superieure des Beaux-Arts, Paris: 17 *centre left*. B.P.K, Berlin/Johannes Laurentius, 1992, Staatliche Museen zu Berlin: 17 *below*. Robert Harding: 20 *top*. 23 *left*, AKG Photo, London: 20 *below*, 22 *right*, The Bridgeman Art Library (BAL): 21 *centre*, 26 *below right*, 27 *top* (BAL/Museum of London), 27 *centre* (BAL/Roger-Viollet, Paris), 31 *top left* (Girandon/BAL), Powerstock Photo Library: 22 *left*, 40 *below right*. Corbis-Bettmann: 30, 31 *top right*, Corbis-Bettmann/UPI 38 *centre right* Victoria & Albert Museum: 31 *centre*. Popperfoto: 31 *below right*, 38 *top, centre left, centre right and below*, 38 *bottom*, 40 *top right*. Courtesy of British Aerospace Military Aircraft: 33, 38 *below centre*, 40 *top left*. Tim Graham: 38 *centre left*; Rex Features: 38 *centre*, 39 *top right, below centre right*. Courtesy of Panasonic: 40 *below left*.

INSIDE BACK COVER: Courtesy of NASA (National Aeronautics and Space Administration).

THE ILLUSTRATED

The Universe   The Solar System   The Story of Life on Earth   Prehistory   The First Cities   Minoan Crete   Troy   Ancient Egypt

WORLD

The Assyrian Empire   Classical Greece   The Roman Empire   The Byzantine Empire   The Crusades   Ming China   Shogun Japan

HISTORY

First Villages of the Americas   The Pueblo Farmers   Empires of the Andes   The Maya   The Incas   The Aztecs   The Viking World

A CHRONICLE FROM THE BEGINNING OF TIME TO THE START OF THE NEW MILLENNIUM

Medieval Christendom   Islamic Empires   The British Empire   World Wars   The Computer Age   Global Information Super-highway

FOREWORD

The Illustrated World History covers the story of life on Earth and continues to the time when historians believed **the earliest civilizations** began, right up to the present day. Since nobody can say how long ago the first year of history was, historians in many civilizations have taken one particular year as a starting point and worked backwards and forwards from there.

The Romans, for example, dated their history from the year in which they believed that the city of Rome had been founded, while **the Muslims** dated theirs from the Hegira, when Mohammed fled from Mecca. (This is indicated by the letters AH, for "after Hegira"). **The Jewish** people reckoned their calendar from 3761 BC, which they believed to be the year of the creation of the world.

The year 0 for this chart and for many countries in the world today is the year in which **Jesus Christ** is said to have been born. The dating system used here is based on **the Gregorian calendar** named after Pope Gregory XIII, which was first introduced in 1582. This calendar makes ordinary years 365 days long, with leap years of 366 days, falling every year in which the date can be divided by four (such as 2000).

INTRODUCTION

The vast panorama of human history will unfold before you in **The Illustrated World History**. The magnificent **timeline**, **key features** and accessible **maps** are sure to excite the curiosity of anyone who desires to learn more.

Hundreds of events, dates and fascinating facts from all around the world are included, accompanied by **hundreds of illustrations** to bring them to life. These are all arranged in coloured bands so you can see what was happening in different places at the same time. **The Illustrated World History** makes learning easy and fun. As the reader will see, the chart is arranged in sections which cover the **historical events** of different parts of the world in the order in which they happened. Below this are the sections devoted to **traders and explorers, scientists and inventors, religion and the arts**. The bottom section gives a bird's-eye view of some of the **firsts in history**.

Perhaps one day some of the young people who read this book will uncover **historical evidence** that overturns the facts given here. It could be that their discoveries will in turn change our views of the past. Views of the past are changing all the time as we find out more. **New historians start here**.

CHRISTOS KONDEATIS

THE BIRTH OF THE UNIVERSE

Our Universe began in a single point about 15 billion years ago. At the Big Bang - the moment of creation - the Universe was concentrated into a single point, infinitely hot and dense. This is the beginning of space and time. Since then the Universe has expanded throughout time to the vastness we can observe today. The farthest objects that astronomers have observed - the superbright cores of distant galaxies called quasars - are about 10 billion light years away.

THE SPEED OF LIGHT

We measure distances in space in terms of the speed of light - the fastest thing known to us. The distance light can travel in a year is about 9.46 thousand billion kilometres. The 'light-year' is the unit used by astronomers to estimate these unimaginable distances. The light from the nearest star, our Sun, takes about 8 minutes and 20 seconds to reach us.

THE MILKY WAY

The Sun is one of 200 billion stars that make up the Milky Way, our home galaxy.

A distant spiral galaxy, similar in structure and contents to our Milky Way

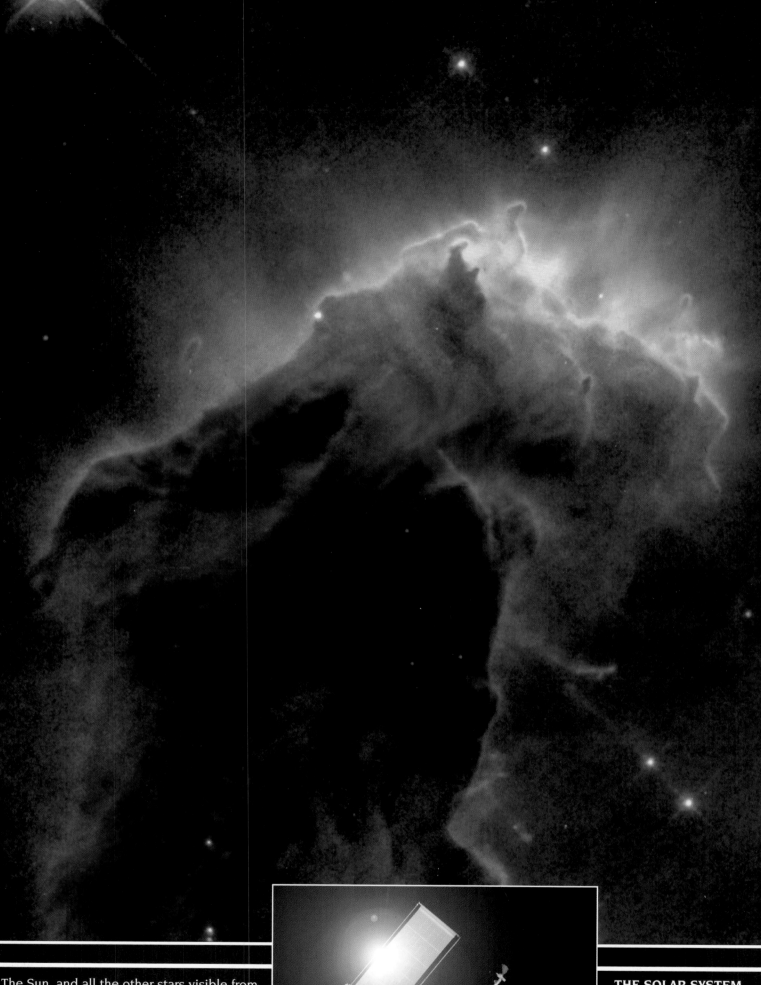

The Sun, and all the other stars visible from Earth in the night sky, belong to our galaxy. The Milky Way is shaped like a giant rotating wheel which bulges in the middle and has spiral arms that contain young stars, bright nebulas and dark clouds of gas and dust. We live near the outer edge of our 12 billion year old galaxy, which is turning on its axis; the Sun takes more than 200 million years to complete a single revolution.
If we could see our galaxy from the outside, it would look like the distant spiral galaxy on the opposite page, below.

THE SOLAR SYSTEM

A spinning cloud of cosmic dust and gas contracted to form a young star, our Sun and its 9 planets, some 4.6 billion years ago. All the planets orbit the Sun in the same direction and are confined more or less to the same plane - Pluto and some comets are the exception. The Earth and the planets rotate on their axes from west to east, unlike Venus and Uranus which spin in the opposite direction. In 1996 NASA scientists found what they believed to be fossil evidence of life on Mars.

OPPOSITE AND ABOVE TOP: **The Hubble Space Telescope** (ABOVE), *photographed these 'deepest-ever' views of the Universe in 1995.*

545-248.2 million years ago

| EVONIAN 417-354 | CARBONIFEROUS 354-290 mya | PERMIAN 290-248 mya | TRIASSIC 248-205.7 million years ago |

MISSISSIPPIAN 354 PENNSYLVANIAN 323

11 *Megazostrodon* 12 *Allosaurus* 13 *Brachiosaurus* 14 *Archaeopteryx* 15 *Stegosaurus* 16 *Triceratops* 17 *Deltatheridium* 18 *Pachycephalosaurus* 19 *Parasaurolo*

SILURIAN 443 mya
With the evolution of **fish with jaws**, the vertebrates make a significant breakthrough. In the late Silurian, the first land plants appear.

DEVONIAN 417 mya
Mollusc
Mountain-building movements reached a peak early in the Devonian, but this was notably a period of explosive evolution. Land was colonized by the earliest **seed ferns**. Fish grew in variety and size,

and the **first land animals** - **amphibians** - evolved.

Fish

CARBONIFEROUS 354 mya
Mountain-building, folding and erosion continued. Forested swamps and deltas in North America and Europe were submerged and formed large coal measures. Glaciation gripped southern continents. **Insects** thrived and the first **reptiles** appeared.

THE DRIFTING CONTINENTS
The continents are drifting very slowly across the Earth's surface, driven by immense heat flows in the semi-molten mantle below. Over millions of years these plates have collided head on, causing land masses to buckle and form mountain ranges. Earthquakes and volcanoes periodically devastate areas where the

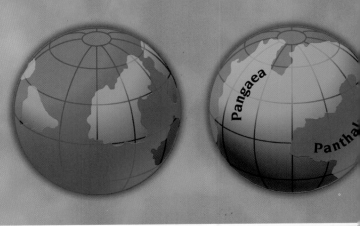

SOLAR SYSTEM   *The relative distances of the planets from the Sun and each other are shown to scale on the diagram above*

PRECAMBRIAN 4600-545 million years ago

PALAEOZOIC

CAMBRIAN 545-495   ORDOVICIAN 495-443   SILURIAN 443-417

1 *Trilobites* 2 *Eusthenopteron* 3 *Ichthyostega* 4 *Meganeura* 5 *Hylonomus* 6 *Dimetrodon* 7 *Eryops* 8 *Coelophysis* 9 *Plateosaurus* 10 *Procompsognathus*

THE STORY OF LIFE ON EARTH

The Primeval Soup
The story of life began about 3.8 million years ago, at a time when the Earth was being bombarded by meteorites and lightning from massive thunderstorms. These inhospitable conditions created the amino acids which became the first building blocks of life.

The age of the Earth that is now accepted by scientists is about 4,600 million years, which is approximately the same as that of the Sun and the rest of the planets.
Single-celled bacteria, the first traces of primitive life, have been found in rocks that are nearly 3,800 million years old - the oldest known rocks on Earth. Before that time the Earth was shaken by frequent earthquakes and

volcanoes, and lacked an adequate atmosphere.
Geologists divide the history of the past into a number of periods. These are:
PRECAMBRIAN 4,600 mya
The greatest section of geological time is represented by the Pre-Cambrian. The **Earth's crust, land masses** and **seas** developed and there was volcanic activity on a massive scale. Precambrian rocks form the great 'shield' areas of all the

continents. Towards the end the Precambrian there are rare traces of soft-bodied animal life.
CAMBRIAN 545 mya This period is the start of the Palaeozoic era and is a time when large numbers of fossils suddenly appear. **Early marine life** became abundant in widespread shallow seas, including animals with hard parts. Marine arthropods, called trilobites, were particularly common.   *Trilobite fossil*

ORDOVICIAN 495 mya
Much of the Earth enjoyed a **mild climate** and seas still covered most of its surface. Layers of sediment continued to be laid down and plate movements pushed up mountain ranges. Common life forms included **reef-building algae, corals, sponges** and **molluscs. Jawless fish,** the first vertebrates (animal with a backbone), made their first appearance.

Cephalopod fossil

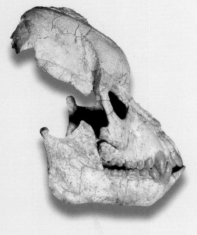

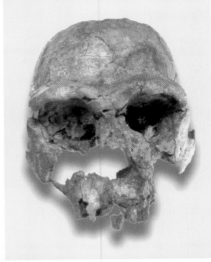

| 23 million years ago | 3-2 million years ago | 2 million years ago | 2.5-1 million years ago |

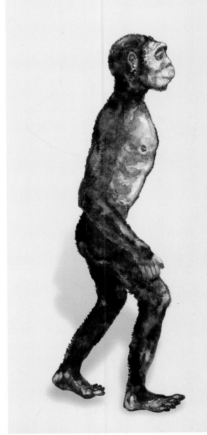

Proconsul

The human story begins in the tropical forests of at least 65 million years ago. By then the first primates, the order of mammals to which humans belong, had appeared. Many of the characteristics that we share with other primates began to develop: sensitive finger pads; binocular vision (3-dimensional vision); and a large brain. This early primate, *Proconsul*, which lived during the *Miocene* (about 23 million years ago) and was about the size of a gibbon, is an early ancestor of the apes and the human family, the hominids.

Australopithecus africanus

Australopithecus africanus ('southern ape of Africa') lived from 3 million to 2 million years ago and probably evolved from *Australopithecus afarensis*. Height: about 1.5m (5 ft). This *hominid*, sometimes known as the 'gracile' or slender *australopithecine* had a body which looked more like a human, although the size of its brain was still fairly small.

Australopithecus robustus

Australopithecus robustus ('robust southern ape') lived about 2 million years ago, dying out 1.2 million years ago. Height: 1.5 - 1.7m (5ft - 5ft 6in). (Sometimes, with *Australopithecus boisei*, called *Paranthropus*.) Both 'robustus' and 'africanus' stood and walked upright. They are not regarded as direct ancestors of modern humans.

Australopithecus boisei

Australopithecus boisei was named after the Englishman *Charles Boise*, who funded excavations in the 1950's. *Australopithecus boisei* lived in East Africa 2.5 million years to 1 million years ago. Height: 1.6m - 1.78m (5ft 2in - 5ft 9in). Also known as '*Nutcracker Man*', because it had huge back teeth.

MESOZOIC 248-65 million years ago

JURASSIC 206-144 million years ago

CRETACEOUS 142-65 million years ago

Pteranodon 21 *Tyrannosaurus Rex* 22 *Glyptodon* 23 *Diatryma* 24 *Hyracotherium* 25 *Moeritherium* 26 *Hyaerodon* 27 *Argentornis* 28 *Indricotherium*

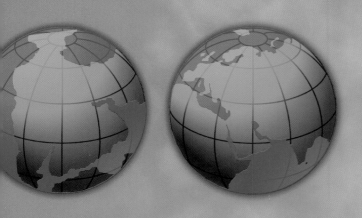

plates grind past one another. 'Plate Tectonics' is the name given to the theory of these massive movements. In 1912, the German meteorologist Alfred Wegener suggested that all of the present continents had at one time been joined in a single supercontinent 270 million years ago. He called the supercontinents Pangaea and the oceans Panthalassa, from the Greek for "all lands" and "all seas".

PERMIAN 290 mya
Desert conditions prevailed over much of Pangaea, the giant land mass made from all the drifting continents. Reptiles spread widely and modern insects *Meganeura* evolved. **New land flora**, including conifers, developed. Then a massive extinction event wiped out 95 per cent of all species.
TRIASSIC 248.2 mya
As the Mesozoic era opened,

Pangaea began breaking up. On land, **conifers** became the dominant plants. This was a *Hylonomus* period of diversity among reptiles, and the **first dinosaurs** and giant forms of marine life appeared. **Primitive mammals** also evolved.
JURASSIC 206 mya Considerable volcanic activity was associated with the opening of the Atlantic Ocean. Dinosaurs reigned on land and **flying reptiles** and **primitive birds** conquered the air. There

30 million years ago   *50 million years ago*

THE STONE AGE

During the Paleolithic era (also called the Old Stone Age) from 2.5-3 million years ago to about 12,000 BC, primitive man was a hunter-gatherer and developed crude stone tools. During the Mesolithic (or Middle Stone Age) which lasted from c 10,000-6000 BC, people began to make tools with handles, called microliths. During the Neolithic, or New Stone Age, (9000-6000 BC in SW Asia, 4000-2400 BC in Europe) people started grow crops and rear animals, and to make tools and weapons of polished stone and flint. By 6000 BC large communities were growing up who lived by subsistence farming. In addition to hunting and fishing, they cultivated wheat and barley and herded sheep and goats.

THE BRONZE AGE

By the beginning of the Bronze Age (c.4500 BC) the ox-drawn plough had replaced the hoe. More efficient farming methods brought increased prosperity and this in turn led to the growth of cities. By 3000, civilizations were growing up where people had specialized occupations, traded, had systems of taxation, developed writing and built large monuments. These early civilizations were mainly in the great river lands of Mesopotamia (Sumer) on the Rivers Tigris and Euphrates, in Egypt along the River Nile, in the Indus Valley and in China between the lower reaches of the Yellow River and the Yangtse. The Egyptian civilization was fully developed by c.3000 BC and other areas of development included the Punjab, the Irawaddy valley, W. Thailand, N. Malaya, Java, The Celebes, the Philippines and Kenya. In the western hemisphere, civilizations were developing in Mesoamerica and the Central Andes. Bronze tools and weapons began to be used at varying stages in different parts of the world, between 3500 and 800 BC. (Some cultures used copper before moving on to bronze.) At the same time, in Europe and Asia, people were trading, reading and writing, and using the wheel and plough.

THE IRON AGE

In about 1500 BC, the Hittites perfected a method for making iron and its use had spread to Europe by the 7th century BC.

THE AMERICAS

Until about 10,000 years ago, people were able to cross the Bering Strait on dry land and had spread to the southern tip of South America before 10,000 BC. Sites were occupied in South and Central America 20,000 years ago, but the earliest well-developed communites date from 10,000-9000 BC. Crops were cultivated perhaps by 6500 BC. By the 1st century BC there were urban societies in the Andes. The Mayan civilization reached its height around AD 300-900 in the Yucatan, with Moche and Nazca states flourishing at the same time. In North America, the Hopewell culture of the Ohio Valley lasted from about 800 BC to AD 400. By 200 BC people were farming in New Mexico and Arizona and this spread to Colorado.

EGYPT

During the 4th millennium small states appeared along the Nile, developed writing and were united under the first dynasty c.3000 BC. The Old Kingdom was a powerful state with a succession of ruling families. At the end of the third millennium, there were conflicts within Egypt, but it united again during the 20th and 19th centuries BC and conquered Nubia, Libya, Palestine and S. Syria. The invading Hyksos ruled for 200 years until they were driven out at the end of the 16th century BC and a New Kingdom was founded. Thutmose III created a new Egyptian Empire in the 14th century, but from the 7th century there were waves of invasions: starting with the Assyrians, followed by the Persians in the 6th century, Alexander the Great in 332 BC and finally Rome in 30 BC.

Perhaps 40,000 years ago

With the end of the last ICE AGE, about 10,000 years ago, new, more northerly lands became available for animals, flora and humans to colonize.

Pueblos

Hopewell

Yucatan Peninsula

Mesoamerican Civilisations

Andean Civilisations

Stonehenge c. 2800 to 1550 BC

CELTS

Etruscans and Rome

CARTHAGE founded by Phoenicians

Gree

EGY

5th century BC Carthaginian Hanno sailed perhaps as far as Cameroon

BANTU

Pyra

ABOVE: Most surviving cave art dates to between 20,000 and 10,000 years ago. The mural art of these hunter-gatherers portrays horses, bison and wild cattle in colourful paintings which may have been done for religious or magical reasons. Most notable are the cave paintings of Lascaux in France and those of Altamira in Spain.

ABOVE: Hunter-gatherer groups at Mezhirich in the Ukraine used mammoth long-bones, skulls, pelvises and vertebrae to construct huts between 18,000 and 12,000 years ago. These dwellings were 4-8 metres in diameter. Animal hides were probably stretched over them.

THE MIDDLE EAST

A favourable climate and good communications helped to make this the 'birth-place' of civilization. The Sumerians were the oldest known urban and literate culture, which began in about 4000 BC. Sargon I conquered the small states of Babylonia in about 2300 BC and founded the kingdom of Akkad. The Old Babylonian Empire reached its peak in c.2150-1740. Among its great kings was Hammurabi, famous for his Code of Laws. Babylonia was conquered by the Assyrians in c.1230 and overthrew the Hittites in c.1200 BC. In the 10th and 9th centuries, the Phoenicians began to colonize the Mediterranean shores as far west as Spain and their colony in Carthage grew strong. Nebuchadnezzar II ruled a New Babylonian Empire which was even more powerful than that of the Assyrians. The next empire to spread across the Middle East was that of the Persians, under

Cyrus the Great, which was in turn conquered by Alexander the Great during the later 4th century.

INDIA

The earliest civlization (c.3000-2000 BC) was the Harappan, which appears to have came to an end as a result of soil erosion, famine and epidemics. In about 800 BC the Ganges alley was colonized and in 322 BC the Mauryan Empire was founded. Its greatest ruler, Asoka, brought the entire subcontinent under his control and Buddhism spread rapidly. The fall of this empire was followed in AD 320 by that of the Guptas who took control of most of north India. The years of peace that followed produced great advances, including decimal numbering using Arabic numerals. The invasion of the White Huns in AD 455 brought the end of the Gupta state, and India split into states which warred with each other for over 500 years.

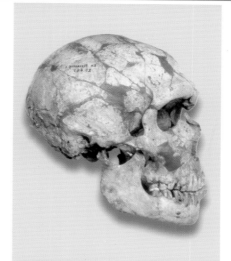
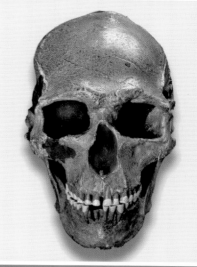

| 2-1.5 million years ago | 1.6-0.5 million years ago | 200,000-35,000 years ago | 30,000 to the present |

Homo habilis

Homo habilis ('Handy man') was the first known species to the genus *Homo* and lived 2 - 1.5 million years ago. Height: 1.2 - 1.5m (4ft- 5ft). *Homo habilis* made simple implements and even used tools for making other tools - hammerstones, for instance - to make sharp flakes. They used tools to skin dead animals but rarely for hunting live game.

Homo erectus

Homo erectus ('Upright man') lived 1.6 million - 500,000 years ago, probably evolving in Africa and spreading to Europe, East Asia and Southeast Asia. Height: 1.5 - 1.8m (5 - 6ft). *Homo erectus* had a larger brain than *Homo habilis*, as well as greater skill at toolmaking. The making of fire was his major technological breakthrough, providing a natural social focus.

Homo sapiens neanderthalensis

Homo sapiens neanderthalensis ('wise Neanderthal man') takes its name from the finds in the Neander Valley in West Germany. The *Neanderthals* lived from about 200,000 to 35,000 years ago. Height; 1.7m (5ft 6in). They were cave-dwellers, made tools and clothes, used fire, may have held ceremonies, and buried their dead. They are not a direct human ancestor.

Homo sapiens sapiens

Homo sapiens sapiens ('the wise, wise man') evolved around 30,000 years ago and is the first fully modern human. Height: 1.69 - 1.77m (5ft 6in - 5ft 8in). The humans' crowning characteristic is intelligence. They carved female figures out of stone and decorated caves with magnificent images of animals. They had become skilled communicators and artists.

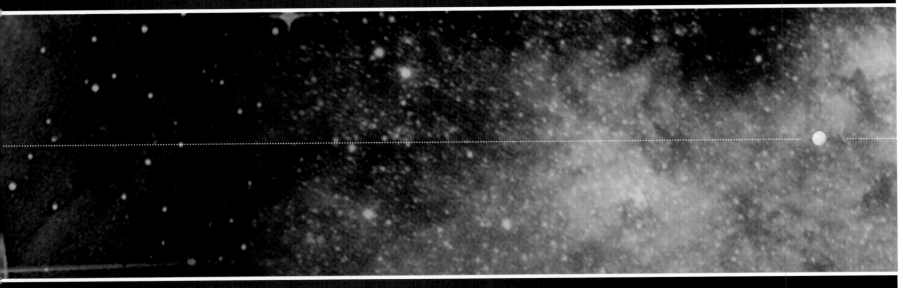

CENOZOIC 65-0.01 million years ago

TERTIARY 65-2 million years ago	QUARTERNARY 1.8

PALEOCENE 65 mya	EOCENE 54.8 mya	OLIGOCENE 33.7	MIOCENE 23.8 mya	PLIOCENE 5.3	PLEISTOCENE	HOLOCENE

29 *Arsinotherium* 30 *Platybelodom* 31 *Mesohippus* 32 *Stenomylus* 33 *Aegyptopithecus* 34 *Megatherium* 35 *Elephant* 36 *Smilodon* 37 *Irish Elk* 38 *Lion*

are traces of the earliest **flowering plants.**
CRETACEOUS 142 mya
Sea-levels rose as the oceans expanded and chalk deposits were laid down, particularly in Britain. Dinosaurs remained dominant until they and many other species were suddenly wiped out by a catastrophic event about 65 mya.
TERTIARY 65 mya
The opening of the Cenozoic (**recent life)** era saw an explosive growth in the number of **mammals.** Many large species evolved,

although others died out. Flowering plants increased rapidly and grasslands appeared as the climate cooled. Vast areas of land were uplifted.
QUATERNARY
1.8 mya
This, the latest geological period, continues up to and including the present day. Four **major ice ages** have alternated with warmer periods. Mammals increased and adapted to climatic change, and **humans evolved to dominate the Earth.**

Deltatheridium

EARTH'S TIME SCALE
If the Earth's existence is thought of as one year long, then the earliest life-forms appeared at the beginning of May. The earliest humans arrived around 7 o'clock in the evening of 31st December , and modern humans evolved at about five minutes to midnight.

EVOLUTION
The naturalist **Charles Darwin** (1809-82) put forward the theory of evolution in his famous work the '*Origin of Species*' (1859). He suggests that animals and plants have evolved from a common ancestor and that increasingly complex organisms have

developed from single-celled organisms.

Darwin calls the process of change natural selection. By this he means that the organisms best suited to their environment are the ones most likely to survive.

ANCIENT CHINA

Farming began between 7000-1700 BC. The Shang Dynasty (1500-1050 BC) was a Bronze Age state with writing, ceremonial rites and specialized labour. The Zhou (or Chou) Dynasty conquered the Shang and established a feudal state. From 771 BC China was broken up into warring states with vast conscript armies. The country was unified in 221 when Shi Huang-ti proclaimed himself Emperor of all China, with standarized written language, roads, canals and uniform coinage, and the Great Wall, built to keep out nomads from the north. After his death in 202 BC, civil war broke out again and continued until the establishment of the Han Dynasty (202 BC-AD 220). China expanded its colonies and improved its communications with countries outside its boundaries, such as the Silk Route linking it with the Roman Empire. A centralized civil service ran the country and Buddhism was introduced. A period of unrest and uncertainty followed, with invasions by nomads who sacked the capital Changan in AD 23 and AD 304. The invasions continued over the next three centuries.

ANCIENT GREECE

BY 3000 BC, there were Mycenaean settlements in Greece and the Minoans on Crete (c.2300-1400 BC) were the earliest advanced civilization in Europe. The Achaeans and Dorians spread widely over the E. Mediterranean and Aegean. Gradually city states began to emerge with colonies in the Aegean, based on sea-borne trade. After 500 BC, Athens was the richest and most culturally advanced Greek state, but the Peloponnesian War with Sparta (461-404 BC) made Greece weaker, which fell before the new power of Macedon. Alexander the Great of Macedon spread Greek culture by conquering the Persian Empire, including Egypt and as far as the Indus. His successors fought each other, until all fell to Rome in the 2nd and 1st centuries BC.

THE ROMAN EMPIRE

By the 3rd century BC Rome headed a powerful Italian confederation, having defeated the Etruscans. After wars with Carthage during the second half of the 3rd century, Rome began to take over the W. Mediterranean and by the end of the 2nd century was controlling Asia Minor. The Roman Republic ended after civil wars in the 1st century BC and Julius Caesar emerged as the leader of the entire Roman world. His heir, Augustus, founded the Empire which flourished for over 200 years. When it began to weaken, Emperor Diocletian (AD 284-305) and Constantine moved the capital to Byzantium, renaming it Constantinople. The Empire continued to be plagued by invasions from tribes like the Vandals, Visigoths, Franks, Burgundians and Ostrogoths, who eventually occupied a large part of the Western Empire. The Emperor in the West was finally deposed in 476, while the Byzantine Empire remained a bastion of Western civilization.

LEFT: *Farmers learned to domesticate animals and by 6000 BC cattle were domesticated in the Sahara region, domesticated sheep first appeared in Iraq about 8700 BC and pigs were first domesticated in Turkey about 7200 BC. As small farming settlements prospered, they built permanent homes, built roads and shops and thus the first seeds of civilization emerged.*

LEFT: *Greek athletes training. Marble relief from the base of a statue of a young man (Kouros), 500 BC, in the National Museum of Athens.*

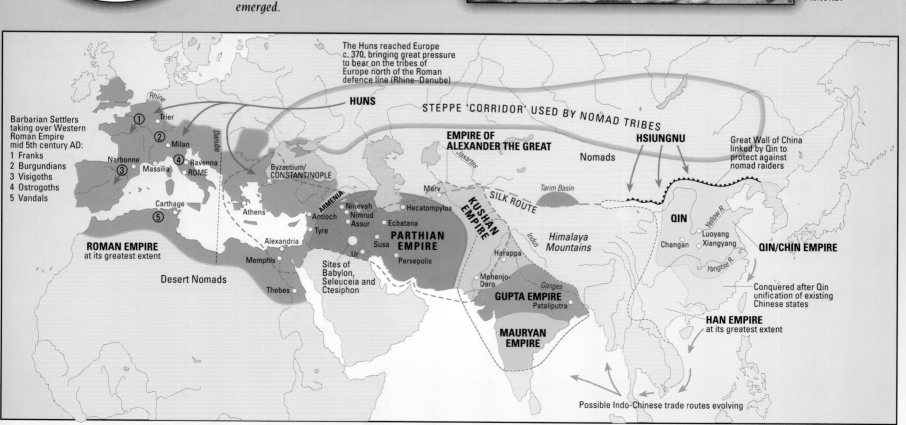

DAWN OF CIVILIZATION

THE AMERICAS

4000 Hunters of North America. Nomads, moving from place to place in search of food, hunt animals and gather wild plants. They use spears and arrowheads made of flint. They also know how to use fire.

3000-2500 Crop Growers of South America. In South and Central America Indians discover how to grow crops, including beans and maize and raise animals for food. People start to build settlements.

2000-1000 Maya of Central America start living in villages.

c.200-1400 Stonehenge, a circle of great stones in England, is built.

EUROPE

4000-3000 Megaliths. In many parts of Europe people build tombs called megaliths, which means "large stones".

2500-2000 The Beaker people. Beaker folk, named after the pottery they bury in graves, travel across Europe and arrive in Britain.

c.2000 Contrasts in Europe. Throughout the Mediterranean areas people develop new skills but Europe is still inhabited by nomads using stone tools.

1400-1200 The Sea Peoples from Greece and the Mediterranean make raids on neighbouring countries looking for places to settle. They destroy the Hittite Empire.

1200 Celtic Ancestors In Northern Europe wandering Urnfield people start to settle and farm in villages.

1200 Trojan Wars involve the rival Greek city states, Troy and Mycenae. According to the poet Homer, Mycenaeans enter the City of Troy hidden in a huge wooden horse, then conquer it.

MIDDLE EAST

c.3000 The First Cities. In Sumer, in southern Mesopotamia ("Land Between the Two Rivers"), rich farming people build some of the world's first cities. Each is part of a city state, ruled by a king, and has a splendid temple made of baked mudbricks.

Sumerian Temple at Ur in Mesopotamia

King Minos and Crete 2000-1450. Minoan civilization with its great palaces flourishes on the Greek island of Crete. Minoans are sailors, traders and craftsmen with their own system of writing (Linear A). During the 1400s their power declines and when Mycenaean people invade, c.1450, their civilization disappears.

1600-1100 Fortress City of Mycenae. A hill-top town with massive walls and a central palace is built, one of many walled towns along the shores of mainland Greece.

Assyrian lion-hunt carving

1814-609 Assyrian Warriors. When Akkad and Babylonia collapse, the Assyrians move in. As their empire grows great, their kings build splendid palaces and make huge wall carvings.

2366-2230 Akkad - The First Empire. King Sargon of Akkad conquers neighbouring Sumer and other lands, bringing a huge "empire" under his rule.

DAWN OF CIVILIZATION

Mesopotamia
China
Egypt
India

c.4000 The first organized groups of people are thought to have lived in four fertile rivers valleys: the Indus in India, between the Tigris and Euphrates in Mesopotamia (Middle East), the Nile in Egypt and the Yellow River in China. As these groups develop, people start to do different jobs, and bring wealth and power to their city states.

Mycenaean burial mask.

2000-1200 Iron People. Hittites, fierce warriors from what is now Turkey, learn to make iron weapons. They keep their new-found skills a secret. In around 1595 they conquer Babylon and for a time they rule lands from the Mediterranean Sea to the Persian Gulf.

David, King of Israel c.1000. By uniting the Kingdoms of Israel and Judah, King David makes his country powerful. His son, Solomon, begins the magnificent temple in Jerusalem to house the sacred Ark of the Covenant.

1122-249 Fierce Chou people overthrow the Shang. They study astronomy and medicine and produce great works of art.

CHINA

1600-1030 The Shang people overthrow the Hsia (possibly the first rulers of China). They farm, build walled towns and make bronzes.

The Iron Age c.1100 Iron weapons and tools are far stronger than those made of bronze. A rapid trade in iron goods develops throughout Europe.

INDIA

c.2500-1750 Cities of the Indus Valley. Kings rule the farming and trading people of the fertile River Indus. Skilled builders construct two famous cities, Mohenjo-daro and Harappa, which are planned like grids.

1500 Aryan Peoples from the north west move into Ganges valley in india.

1991-1786 Egypt's Middle Kingdom. The pharaohs rule well, and build a splendid new royal city at Thebes. They receive a setback when the Hyksos people invade.

1567-1085 Egypt's New Kingdom. The most glorious time in Egypt's history begins after the Hyksos are driven out. The Pharaohs plan mighty buildings such as the magnificent temples built by Rameses II at Abu Simbel, which are cut out of rock.

AFRICA

Great Kingdom of Egypt 3100-1085. In 3100 the first pharaoh (King), Menes, joins the two countries of North and South Egypt. Mathematicians, doctors, artists, engineers and builders enrich life in the Egyptian Kingdom. Pharaoh rule lasts for 2500 years.

c.2773 Egyptians use calendar with 365 days.
c.2700 Chinese make silk from the cocoons of silkworms.
c.2500-2350 Babylonians study the stars.
c.2500 Central Asian people tame horses.
c.2500 Mesopotamians begin measuring length, weight and volume in units.
c.2500 Egyptians perform surgery.

2686-2181 Age of the Pyramids. Egyptian believe their pharaohs to be sons of Ra, the Sun god and build magnificent tombs, called pyramids, to honour them. They preserve the bodies of their dead by mummifying them.

1503-1483. Egyptian Queen Hatshepshut's reign heralds a great time to trade, with expeditions to Punt in Africa.

1200-800 Phoenician Seafarers. Phoenician seafarers are merchants sail the Mediterranean, setting up ports and trading posts. They also travel as far as the Atlantic Ocean and down West Africa's coast. Among their cities are Sidon and Tyre, famous for purple dye. They trade in glass, purple cloth and metal goods.

c.3600 Mesopotamians use the stone potter's wheel and the wooden cartwheel.

3500 Egyptians use metal mirrors.
c.3000 Egyptians use oxen to pull their ploughs.

c.3000 Sumerians divide the day into 24 hours, 60 minutes, 60 seconds and a circle into 360 degrees.
c.3000 Sumerians fill bad teeth.

2650 Great architect and doctor Imhotep, is involved in the building of the Step Pyramid for King Zoser.

2350 Great Pyramid of Cheops takes 20 years to build, using millions of stone blocks.

c.1340 In Egypt's famous Valley of the Kings, the body of the boy-king Tutankhamen is buried with fabulous treasures.

1500-600 Growth of Hindu religion, which teaches that everything is part of a single world spirit.

1200 A great poem tells the adventures of Gilgamesh, a Sumerian King.

Early Writing c.3100 Sumerians begin to write using picture language. Then they develop a shorter form called cuneiform script using wedge-shaped marks on pieces of clay. The Egyptians start to use picture writing, called hieroglyphics, and also invent a type of paper made from the papyrus reed.

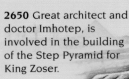

Pyramids and Sphinx at Giza, one of the Seven Wonders of the ancient world.

c.3000 Pharoah Atothis writes first book on human body.

c.2296 Chinese are the first to record sighting of a comet.

Portrait of Tutankhamen

c.2200 Queen Semiramis of Babylon builds first tunnel below a river.

c.1800 Babylonians use multiplication tables.

c.2000 First zoo opens in China.

1200 Jews begin their worship only one god, Jahweh.

0 First Known American ...zation Olmec Indians live ...d the Gulf of Mexico. ...write, use numbers, and ...great sculptures.

500BC-AD250 Native American Hunters stalk and trap buffaloes for their meat and skins.

Great Age of Athens 479-338
After the Persian defeat in 480, Athens is rebuilt and becomes the most powerful city in Greece. One of it's greatest leaders is Pericles (r.443-429).

Athens overlooked by the Parthenon.

Pericles

300BC-600AD Zapotec Tribes living around Monte Alban in southern Mexico worship the rain god.

...irth of Rome. ...e north of the Alps ... into Italy and ...by the River Tiber. ...d tells that Romulus ...emus, nursed by a she-wolf, are ...'s founders.

c.700-400 Etruscans from central Italy take over neighbouring lands and make fine cities. They are skilled metal-workers and busy traders and also know how to drain land for growing crops. From 600-200 the Etruscans rule Rome.

c.510-509 The Roman Republic. People of Rome rise against their King, Tarquin the Proud, and set up a "public state" or republic.

c.600 Spartan Soldier State. Sparta is a very severe city state in Greece which trains even its youngest citizens to serve the state. The Spartans despise the arts and shun comfort. They also force large numbers of slaves to work for them.

400 Sacred Geese of Rome. When the French Gauls move south and sack Rome, only the citadel on a high hill escapes, saved, it is said, by a warning from geese.

500-200 Celtic Tribes, sometimes living in hillforts, spread over most of Europe, but never become a united nation. These people are warlike as well as artistic.

338 Greek Unity. Philip II of Macedonia, in northern Greece, unites the country by defeating all city states except Sparta.

264 First Punic War. This breaks out between Rome and Carthage, trade rivals in the Mediterranean. In the first war Rome wins Sicily.

Greek City States ...er and grow strong ...after an age of ...ct.

...f Democracy 600-500 Greek citizens begin to overthrow their kings. Around the year 500 they create a government by free men, with an elected assembly, and "democracy" in a limited sense is born.

Aegean Sea *Troy* *Athens* *Mycenae* *Crete*

490-480 Greeks Defeat Persians at the battle of Marathon to free the Greek colonies. Xerxes, the next Persian King, then invades Greece and according to legend, overcomes 300 Spartans, who fight to the death to hold the pass of Thermopylae. Xerxes' fleet is finally defeated at the Battle of Salamis.

Alexander the Great r.336-323. At the age of 20, Philip of Macedonia's son becomes King. Taught by the scholar Aristotle, he is a great warrior and empire builder, and his first victories are against Persia and Egypt, 333-331. In an attempt to conquer the world, he marches with his army to India but his soldiers become so exhausted that they demand to return home. Alexander still manages to build a vast empire, founding many cities and declaring that all races shall be equal.

264-236 Asoka Emperor of India. A devout Buddhist, Asoka sends missionary priests around his huge empire. He one of India's greatest rulers.

...n Empire 546-334. ...r its ruler Cyrus II ...-529) the Persian ...re grows very large ...ring today's Iran ...fghanistan). Cyrus ...s both the King of ..., and King Croesus ...ia, and captures ...on in 538. In 520 ...ccessor Darius I ...to build the great ...l city of Persepolis ...xtend the empire ...rther.

926 Kingdom of Israel divides again.

INDIA
321 Northern India Unites under Chandragupta Maurya. His Empire will stretch from Bengal to the Afghan borders.

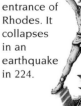

People of Chavin ...uantar in ...s in Peru make ...tiful gold objects.

605-562 Strong ruler Nebuchadnezzar II extends his empire and creates the Hanging Gardens of Babylon.

481-221 Warring states of China. Seven large states fight during this period.

722-464 "Spring and Autumn" Period. China is still a collection of numerous states, usually at war.

China's First Empires 221BC-9AD. Ch'in State conquers other states in China. The Emperor, Shi Huang Ti, gives orders to destroy many books. In 202 the Han overthrow Shi Huang Ti and make their leader, Liu Pang, Emperor. A time of peace and great scientific progress follows. People must take exams to obtain government jobs. In 140-87 Han Emperor, Wu Ti, brings Chinese power to Central Asia and rules millions of people.

332 Great City of Egypt. Alexander the Great invades Egypt and founds Alexandria.

300 Bantu People spread over east and southern Africa.

332 Alexandria, Egypt, becomes a centre of learning, with a marvellous library and museum.

306-283 Euclid, the world's most famous mathematician, writes his great book *The Elements.*

264 The Port of Adulis in Ethopia where Africa and Arabia meet, becomes a world trade centre. Cinnamon and frankincense arrive from Arabia, silks and spices from India, wrought iron from Kush, timber and ivory from Ethopia itself, and European goods.

264-100 Pirates wreck Mediterranean trade.

814 Powerful Carthage. Phoenicians from Syria build Carthage in North Africa, and trade with Africans for gold. The city becomes a major trading centre.

610-545 Thales, a Greek philosopher, teaches the importance of using reason and observation to understand the world.

530 Pythagoras, a great Greek mathematician, influences the development of maths and shows its importance in astronomy.

Pottery Army of Shi Huang Ti

460 The "Father of Medicine", Greek doctor Hippocrates, teaches that a body can heal itself with rest and simple foods. The Hippocratic Oath, which doctors take today, is based on his original principles.

Homer, a Greek ...writes the *Iliad* and ...*dyssey,* poems ...t the Trojan Wars.

-400 Great religious ...gs, the *Upanishads,* ...ar in India.

-500 Early period ...eek art, called ...aic", is famous for ...tiful sculptures of ...s and young girls.

First coins used ...dia (Turkey).

Symbol for zero is ...entioned in India.

Work begins on ...rst Suez Canal.

639 Library at Nineveh contains over 22,000 clay tablets on many subjects.

c.600 Aesop probably a freed slave, becomes famous for his fables.

551 Birth of Confucius, the great Chinese philosopher. He teaches that others should be treated as you would like to be treated yourself.

c.580-563 Birth of Buddha. Prince Siddhartha Gautama founds the Buddhist religion and states that only those who obey his teachings can escape life's pain and sufferings.

c.605-531 Birth of Lao-Tze, founder of Taoism, who teaches that people should lead a simple honest life.

500 Chinese use coins shaped like knives, spades and discs.

480 Sea captain, Hanno of Carthage, explores the coast of West Africa.

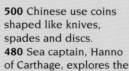

c.300 Delphic Oracle. Legend tells us that the decisions of important leaders are guided by the advice of the oracle at this famous site.

500-200 Nok culture in central Nigeria produces skilful iron sculptures of men and beasts.

c.400 Democritus, a Greek philosopher, suggests that the world is made up of tiny particles called atoms.

c.300 Gods of Rome. Early Roman gods include gods of nature and other "minor" gods, and personal gods of the household.

c.450 Herodotus of Halicarnassus, "The Father of History", writes first great world history. Greek philosophers look for explanations for why humans are as they are and set up schools. But in 399, the philosopher Socrates is condemned to death for his ideas.

Wonders of the Ancient World 433 massive statue of Zeus, King of the Greek gods, is built for the temple of Olympia.

300-280 The Colossus of Rhodes is a huge statue of Helios the sun god built at the harbour entrance of Rhodes. It collapses in an earthquake in 224.

Classical Age in Greece 500-338. Greeks lead the world in art, architecture, literature, politics, philosophy and science. Large open air theatres show plays by Aeschylus, Sophocles and other great writers. The Greeks believe that music, song and dance benefit both mind and body.

Plato

Greek Gods. Greeks worship many gods, believed to live on Mount Olympus. Myths tell of their deeds

First Olympic ...s held in honour ...us in sacred site ...ympia in the ...tains of Greece.

c.556-539 Nabonidus, King of Babylon, is the first known archaeologist.

500 First record of the use of the bow and arrow in North America. The Inuit (Eskimos) may have brought bows and arrows from Asia.

450-200 Celtic "La Tene" culture produces fine works of art and crafts. Their armour, tools and ornaments are very beautiful.

c.390 Legendary Chinese artist makes a kite.

420 Primary schools are created in Athens. They are for boys from powerful families only.

THE AMERICAS **200 Mayan Tribes** start to settle in the jungles of Central America.

c.100 Basket Makers of North America. People in the south west live as farmers.

Timeline continues on page 18

EUROPE

218 Hannibal Crosses the Alps. Second Punic War sees Carthage's spectacular general, Hannibal, leading his army and 37 elephants from Spain, through the snow-covered Pyrenees and Alps into Italy. He wins three battles aginst the Romans. Later, in defeat, he kills himself rather than be taken prisoner.

The Roman Empire 264BC-AD250. The Roman army, with its well trained troops, sweeps through a great part of the known world. Romans are most efficient rulers, building towns and cities and thousands of miles of excellent roads, and introducing laws.

149-146 Third Punic War. Rome crushes Carthage. Men, women and children are sold into slavery.

133-122 Rome's Civil War. Rome is rocked by almost a century of civil war following the murder of the Gracchi brothers who demanded government changes.

215 Great Wall of China.
CHINA Northern Tartars are kept out by a wall 1,500 miles long.

73 The Slaves' Revolt. Led by Spartacus and other escaped gladiators, their army swells to over 100,000 men before they are defeated.

63 Palestine becomes a Roman province.

53-44 Julius Caesar becomes the Romans' greatest leader. In 45 Caesar becomes sole ruler of the empire but a year later, on the Ides of March, he is murdered.

AD43 Romans invade Britain. Disciplined Roman army marches northward through Britain and defeats local tribes. Celtic chieftain, Caractacus, tries to resist them but is defeated. The Romans then rule Britain for nearly 400 years, renaming it Britannia.

65 Chariot Races. Julius Caesar, in charge of public games, arranges great spectacles which ensure his popularity.

64 Nero. During Nero's rule much of the city of Rome burns to the ground in a great fire.

40-4 King Herod the Great, ruler of Judaea, brings his country under Roman rule. According to the Gospel he is cruel and ruthless. When told of the birth of Jesus Christ, he orders the deaths of all baby boys, to ensure that the new "king" is killed.

70 Jewish Rebellion takes place against the Romans in Judaea. The Jews are forced, for the first time, to leave their homeland.

14-37 Rome's Second Emperor, Tiberius, makes himself unpopular by accusing many people of treason.

37-41 Caligula. Once a good Roman ruler, Caligula becomes insane, making a horse a consul.

27 Octavian, heir to Julius Caesar, takes the name "Augustus", becomes first Emperor of Rome and brings peace.

r.98-117 Trajan. The Roman Empire is at its peak at around 116, under Emperor Trajan, who successfully extends his empire to the east.

79 Pompeii Destroyed. Vesuvius, a volcano in Italy, erupts and buries Pompeii, preserving it for future generations.

117-138 Hadrian looks after Empire's defences. He has Hadrian's Wall built in 122 to stop the raiding Picts of Scotland from invading Britain.

Octavian, known as Augustus

100s Roman trading posts extend fron the south west coast of India to southern edge of the Sahara. Grain, oil, silks, spices, pottery, stone, jewellery and textiles, fill the warehouses of Rome.

AFRICA   51-30 Cleopatra, Queen of Egypt is joint ruler of Egypt from 51, and mistress of Julius Caesar and Mark Antony. When Octavian conquers Egypt, Antony and Cleopatra commit suicide. It is said that Cleopatra uses a poisonous snake.

c.90 Merchants carrying precious silk begin to travel along a great 2,500 mile trade route, known as "the Silk Road",

c.250 Archimedes, a Greek mathematician and engineer, outlines the laws of specific gravity.

202BC-AD9 During the great Han Dynasty, the Chinese invent paper, make gunpowder and invent movable type. They also make discoveries in engineering, acupuncture and astronomy.

246 Chinese engineers complete the Chengkuo Canal, one of many irrigation schemes for controlling floods in China.

279 The Pharos of Alexandria is a great light house built by Sostratus.

c.200 *The Mahabharata*, an Indian poem, 18 books long, is written.

270-230 Ctesbius of Alexandria invents the organ, water pump, spring and valve.

270 Greek astronomer Aristarchus states that the Earth revolves around the Sun.

c.AD150 Ptolemy of Alexandra, brilliant mathematician, astronomer and geographer, writes his famous book, *Geography*, used in schools for hundreds of years.

500BC-250AD Great builders of Rome construct thousands of miles of roads, tunnels, aqueducts, public buildings, bridges and canals throughout their empire.

31BC-14AD Augustan Age in Rome is a time of peace which encourages literature and poetry, including the works of Ovid, Horace and Virgil.

47 The New Year starts on January 1 for the first time. This Roman calendar is introduced by Julius Caesar.

Life of Christ c.4BC-AD30. Jesus Christ, founder of Christianity, preaches throughout Judaea, telling people to love one another. He gathers many disciples around him and explains to them that he is the *"Son of God"*.

79 First known "Beware of the Dog" sign: *cave canem*. It is found in floor mosaic in Pompeii.

80 Cement and concrete used in building of the Colosseum in Rome.

147 In Han China, Prince Liu Sheng is buried in a suit of 2,498 jade pieces.

30 Christianity spreads throughout the Roman Empire after the death of Christ, particularly when Paul of Tarsus stops his persecution of Christians and becomes a fearless and devout Christian missionary.

60 Buddhism reaches China from Central Asia and India.

105 The Chinese use paper which is made of vegetable fibres.

100 Italy first uses under-floor heating.

The Colosseum

4000BC TO AD250 ~ GREAT CIVILIZATIONS

EGYPT AND THE PHARAOHS

The pharaohs' rule was to last for 2,500 years. During the Age of the Pyramids, from 2686 to 2181BC, the Egyptians built magnificent tombs to honour their pharaoh kings - believing them to be the sons of Ra, the sun god. Bodies were preserved by mummification and placed in elaborate painted coffins called sarcophagi. Later, in about 1340BC, Egypt's most famous boy king, Tutankhamen, was buried in an immense shrine in the Valley of the Kings. This shrine was full of fabulous treasure: jewellery, chairs, chariots and caskets - much of it in gold.

A powerful and cultured civilization, the Egyptians were clever mathematicians, builders, engineers, doctors and artists, who created magnificent architecture, introduced the 365-day calendar, performed exact surgical operations and developed the use of writing materials, from animal skin parchment to an early kind of paper made from the papyrus reed.

When a sacred animal died it wa mummified and buried in a specia cemetery.

The Great Pyramid

• The Great Pyramid at Giza on the edge of Cairo in Egypt is the only surviving ancient wonder of the world.

• Some mystics believe that the stones which are missing from the very top of the Pyramid may have been made of gold.

• When all the stones were in place, the Pyramid would have been higher than the spire of Salisbury Cathedral and the dome of St Paul's in London.

• The Pyramid contains about 2.5 million blocks of limestone. Some of the larger blocks weigh 15 tonnes each. The total weight would be about 6 million tonnes.

• It is believed that 4000 builders and masons would have taken 20 to 30 years to build the Great Pyramid.

• It was completed over 4000 years ago.

• The building occupies a total area of 13 acres (5.3 hectares).

THE MINOANS OF CRETE

From 2000 to 1450BC the Minoan civilization, with its great palaces and fine paintings, flourished in the island of Crete. Excellent sailors, traders and craftsmen, the Minoans dominated the Mediterranean at that time and captured many slaves. This, along with their worship of the bull - shown in many of their wall paintings and works of art - may have given rise to the Greek legend of Theseus and the Minotaur in the labyrinth.

The Minoans developed their own system of writing (called Linear A and Linear B) which is similar to, but not the same as, Egyptian hieroglyphics. However, eventually their power declined when the Mycenean people began to invade Crete successfully. By about 1450BC the rich Minoan civilization had disappeared.

A wall painting (fresco) of dolphins from the Queen's apartment in the Minoan palace at Knossos, Crete, dating from the 16th century BC.

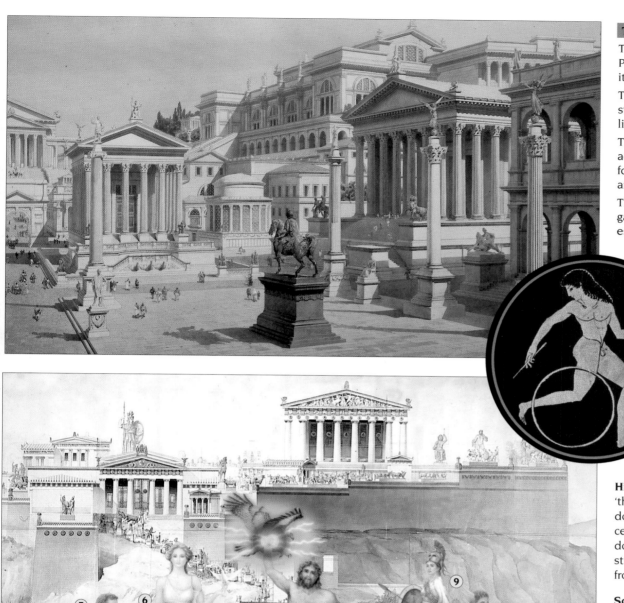

THE ROMAN EMPIRE

The Roman Empire lasted for over four centuries. Powered by its enormous army of well-trained troops, it swept through most of the then known world.

The Romans were efficient rulers who created well-structured towns and cities wherever they went, linked by a network of excellent roads.

They introduced laws, new farming methods, aqueducts to transport water to their cities, an early form of central heating and the Roman letters which are used throughout most of the Western world today.

They built vast arenas in which to hold their public games and spectacles such as chariot races and, especially as their empire began to decline, some very bloodthirsty sports involving human victims.

FAR LEFT: A watercolour reconstruction of the Roman Forum

Illustrations of children's games, such as this boy rolling a hoop, appear on vases.

SOME FACTS ABOUT FAMOUS GREEKS

Aesop was a slave from Thrace who was set free by his master, Iadmon. Although he is famous as a teller of moral tales about animals, the fables as we know them today were probably compiled in medieval times.

Hippocrates, born on the island of Kos, is known as 'the father of medicine'. He was certainly a renowned doctor and the ideals in the Hippocratic oath have for centuries been regarded as the correct ones for doctors to follow - so much so that some medical students today still use the oath when graduating from university or medical school.

Socrates was a great philosopher from Athens. He did not record his ideas himself but we have learned about them through the works of others, including Plato. At the age of 70, for political reasons, Socrates was convicted of corrupting the young and neglecting the gods and was sentenced to death. Offered the chance to think of an alternative punishment, he suggested that he might be allowed to live for the rest of his life, supported by public money and offered to pay a very small fine. An angry court duly sentenced him to death by drinking the poison hemlock.

GREEK AND ROMAN GODS

The Romans were inventive and very good at using other people's ideas, adapting them to fit into their own way of life. They learned a good deal from the countries they conquered and from what had happened before their arrival. They then took this knowledge with them as their empire extended, spreading the ideas and information to most of the known western world. For example, they adopted the Greek gods, giving them their own names. Quite a few of the words we use today are derived from the names of these gods.

	Greek name	Roman name	Responsibilities
1	Hera	Juno	Queen of heaven; marriage and motherhood
2	Zeus	Jupiter	Father of gods and men; justice and virtue
3	Poseidon	Neptune	earthquakes and water; the sea
4	Hephaestus	Vulcan	fire and furnace; smiths and craftsmen
5	Artemis	Diana	the moon; chastity
6	Aphrodite	Venus	love and fertility; beauty
7	Ares	Mars	war; agriculture, flocks and herds
8	Hermes	Mercury	message carrying; taking the dead to Hades; trade
9	Athena	Minerva	war; wisdom; arts and crafts
10	Apollo	Phoebus	prophecy
11	Dionysus	Bacchus	wine and pleasure-loving
12	Demeter	Ceres	cornfield and Spring

ABOVE: A watercolour reconstruction of the Acropolis at Athens. In the foreground, the 12 Olympian gods. The ancient Greeks believed that their gods lived on the lofty summit of Mount Olympus which reached right into heaven. The first god in the sky, called Uranus, married the earth goddess, Gaea. Zeus, son of Cronus, was their grandson.

Pythagoras, who is perhaps best known for his geometry and arithmetic theorems, was also one of the first people to believe that the earth and the universe were spherical, and to discover the musical octave.

Pythagoras' theorem: the square on the hypotenuse of a right-angled triangle is equal to the sum of the squares on the other two sides.

DID YOU KNOW THAT...

• Tutankhamen became king of Egypt when he was only 10. He married a girl of 12 and died when he was only about 19 years old. His coffin was made of solid gold, weighing 240 lbs (110 kg).

• The Olympic Games began in 776 BC. In the first Olympic Games all the athletes were naked. Even in wrestling matches, they were classified not by weight but by age alone and had to compete against others in the categories of boy, adolescent and man.

• In the Roman games, elephants were trained to kneel in front of the Emperor's box and write Latin in the sand with their trunks. Sometimes the amphitheatres were flooded to stage mock battle scenes at sea or fights with crocodiles.

RIGHT: Schoolmasters (Pedagogues) taught letters, arithmetic and music in Greek schools.

THE AMERICAS

300-600 City of the Gods. Huge city-state of Teotihuacán flourishes in Mexico. An amazing city of pyramids, it covers eight square miles and has twenty-three temples. People worship Quetzalcoatl, the feathered serpent god.

300-500 Great Mounds of North America. Hopewell Indians make huge animal-shaped mounds.

200-600 Moche People in Peru make fine pottery and sculpture.

Great Serpent Mound in Ohio

EUROPE

Constantine the Great c.274-337 reunites the Roman Empire, allows people to be Christians and becomes, on his deathbed, the first Christian Roman Emperor.

330 He establishes a new capital of Constantinople, now known as Istanbul.

MIDDLE EAST

55-641 New Persian Empires gradually grows rich from trading between the East and West. In 641 the empire falls to the Muslim Arabs.

INDIA

Great Gupta Empire 320-535 Chandragupta, (r.320-335), founder of the Hindu Gupta Dynasty, unites northern India and oversees a great age of arts, medicine and mathematics. Samudragupta, (r.335-375), tolerant "poet king", rules one of the largest empires India has ever seen. Chandragupta II rules peacefully from 375-415.
465 This Empire breaks apart.

AFRICA

c.100 Mountain Kingdom of Axum, Ethiopia grows rich from ivory trade. Many palaces and temples are built.

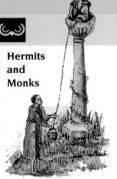
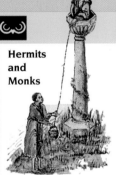

Hermits and Monks

305 St Antony organizes a group of Christian hermits, into a kind of monastery.
c.400-500 Hermit's Choice. One hermit, St Simeon, lives for many years on top of a pillar. His food is sent up to him in a basket.
526 First Monastery. Monte Cassino, Italy, is founded by St Benedict.

c200-300 Wheelbarrows used in China.
270 The Chinese use a magnetic compass.

CHINA

300-350 Age of Confusion. Northern horsemen invade, breaking through the Great Wall in 304 and sacking the capitals of Loyang and Cangan.

330 Axum is converted to Christianity.
330 Axum conquers neighbouring Kush.
380 Roman Emperor Theodosius closes pagan temples in Egypt, and destroys idols.

c.300-700 Mayan priests are interested in the concept of time. They develop accurate calendars and calculate how long the sun's year is.

300 Chinese use stirrups when riding.
350 Sawmill used in France for cutting marble.
c.350 Public hospital opens in Rome.

400-500s Britain Conquered. After Roman troops leave Britain, Angles, Saxons and Jutes settle there.
476 Barbarian Kingdoms are now set up in Europe.
481 Clovis Becomes King of the Franks in Gaul and converts to the Christian religion.
451 Huns from the East led by Attila, invade Gaul, and attack northern Italy in 452.

Barbarian Menace and the fall of Rome 370-476 Fierce Germanic tribes from Scandinavia and Asia attack the Empire's borders. They are called Barbarians. The most serious invasion, which finally destroys the empire, are carried out by:
410 Germanic Visigoths, led by Alaric, sack and loot Rome.
455 Germanic Vandals who sack Rome.

The Messenger of Gods c.570-631 Mohammed, prophet of the religion of Islam, begins to preach in Mecca, 613. He dictates the Koran, which means "Divine Word", to his followers, the Muslims, in 625, and lays down many rules for everyday life.

400 Feudal Japan. A rich feudal society starts to develop.
ASIA
429 Powerful Vandals set up kingdoms in North Africa
400-500 Indian mathematicians invent symbols for zero, decimal numbers and Arabic numbers.

c.350-550 This is the Great Age of Gupta in India, where beautiful temple cave paintings show the splendid courts of India's rulers.

Early Christian Missionaries 432-590
432 St Patrick travels from Britain to convert the Irish to Christianity.
550 St David takes Christianity to Wales.
590 Gregory the Great reluctantly becomes Pope, helps the poor and sends missionaries to barbarian tribes.
596 St Augustine is sent by Gregory to convert the English to Christianity. The pagan festival, Christmas Day, is transformed into a Christian one, which celebrates the birth of Christ.
c.560-900 Monasteries become major centres of learning and art.

Mayan Golden Age 300-600 Mayan people of Central America live in huts and farms over large areas. They worship the rain god and make sacrifices, sometimes human. Their priests study the heavens, use picture writing and are clever mathematicians. People play religious ball games on special courts, using hip and elbow bones to hit the ball.

476 Roman Empire Breaks up as the last Roman Emperor, Augustus, is deposed.
500 Battle of Mount Badon is the last of twelve great battles against the Saxons. Legend tells us that King Arthur fought in this Battle.
546 Ostrogoths capture Rome after a year's siege. Romans are forced to flee from there city.

The Spread of Islam 622 Mohammed, opposed by rich merchants, flees from Mecca, but captures it in 630. He defeats nomads at the Battle of Hunayn in 631, and unites fighting tribes. Inspired by the teachings of Islam, Muslims sweep into the Middle East, Asia, North Africa and Europe.

589 Sui Dynasty unites many Chinese states.
624 Buddhism becomes state religion in China.
618-907 Age of Tang. A united country brings a time of wealth, and the arts flourish until, around 755, China begins to split into different states.

594 Buddhism becomes Japan's state religion.

c.600 The Sahara Crossing. Caravans of camels brave the desert crossing to take goods south into the heart of Africa. They return with gold, leather, kola nuts and slaves.

605-610 Millions of Chinese work on the Imperial Canal.

537 The magnificent church of Hagia Sophia, in Constantinople, becomes the centre of the Christian world.

692 The first great Islamic building, Dome of the Rock in Jerusalem, is finished.

Early Middle Ages in Europe c.500-1000
Europe is left in chaos after the fall of Rome. In the Western Empire people are desperately poor and lose interest in learning.

c.600 Tiahuanoco Temples. Temples are built in the Bolivian Andes with a massive "Gateway of the Sun".

871-899 Alfred the Great, Saxon King of Wessex stops Danish Vikings from taking England.

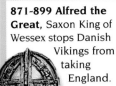
Anglo-Saxon helmet buried at Sutton Hoo, England

Byzantine Empire 420s-1453
520s Constantinople becomes capital of the eastern half of the former Roman Empire.
527-565 Justinian, intelligent Byzantine Emperor, reconquers the Western Empire, rebuilds Constantinople and brings Roman law up to date. His powerful wife, Theodora, helps him to rule. The Roman Empire collapses but the Byzantine Empire lasts for 1,000 years. Later it declines as a result of treachery and invasion.
886 Michael "The Drunkard" is killed by his groom, who becomes the first of several strong rulers.

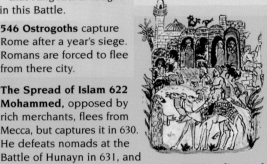

732 Islamic Advance Halted in Europe. Frankish General Charles Martel, ("The Hammer") stops the invasion of France by Arabs, also known as Moors, at the Battle of Poitiers.
756 Syrian Poet Prince Abd al-Rahman sets up Muslim state in Spain.

661-750 Muslim Arab Empire, ruled by the Omayyads, influences one third of the world.
750 Abbasids, who claim descent from Abbas, Mohammed's uncle, kill the Omayyads and establish Baghdad, a brilliant cultural centre.

750 Three Empires of India are at war with each other. Muslim Arabs begin to invade the River Indus area.

645-784 Chinese Influence. The Japanese admire "Chinese" style and start to copy Chinese buildings, art and writing.

751 Islamic Influences The Arab Muslims crush Chinese armies on the River Talis, making a way for Islam spread though central Asia.

700 Swedish Vikings settle on the shores of the Baltic.

813-833 Mamum the Great sets up a learning centre to bring knowledge of the Ancient World to Arabia.
865-925 Rhazes, chief doctor of the Baghdad Hospital, studies disease.

Illustration from the Book of Kells

700-750 The *Lindisfarne Gospels* and the Irish *Book of Kells* are created.
715 *Beowulf,* the first English epic poem, that tells of a warrior's struggle against dragons and monsters, is written.
726-843 Byzantine Emperor Leo III bans worship of icons.
712-770 Golden Age of Chinese poetry. Today 49,000 poems still exist.
805 Charlemagne's Palace Chapel at Aachen is declare to be sacred.
764-809 Rule of Hueum al-Rashid whose court is mad famous in *The Arabian Nights.*

c.750 The Chinese invent a mechanical clock powered by a water wheel.
800 In Western Europe, modern musical notation begins.

500-1200 Hohokam Indians, who inhab south-west part of N America, build larg irrigation channels make colourful pot

He defeats them at Edington in 878, but allows the Danes to k East Anglia and Mer on the understandin that their King, Guth becomes a Christian Alfred then builds a powerful navy to def against further Dani invasions. He is a go and learned ruler an

Charlemagne, King the Franks 724-81 A determined Fram King, Charlemagne fights to extend his kingdom in northern

c.800 Slav Tribes o Eastern Europe unite under rule of Viking warrior merchants fro Sweden, known as the "Rus".
850 First Russian States are founde
898 Hungary foun
929 "Good King Wenceslas" Christian ruler of Bohemia, is murdered by his pagan brother. H becomes a saint.

700-875 Vikings fr Norway and Denm move west and cr the Atlantic Ocean Iceland, Greenland and America

980-1037 Avicenna, Persian doctor, write the famous *Canon* of medicine.
900 China sees a gr age of iron and stee
932 Chinese mass produce books. The use wood blocks for printing.

868 A printed book *Diamond Sutra,* is ma in China, using woo blocks for printing

Mayas of Yucatan move the Yucatan peninsula.

980 Toltec Warriors ...de Mayan centres and ...e Tula their capital.

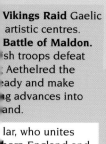

Vikings Raid Gaelic artistic centres.

Battle of Maldon. ...sh troops defeat ...Aethelred the ...ady and make ...g advances into ...and.

...lar, who unites ...hern England and ...slates many Latin ...ks into English.

...Germany and ...gary and prevent the ...ntine Empire from ...ming too strong. He ...fights Muslim Arabs ...Moors) in Spain and ...ures Barcelona. He ...urages new interest ...arning and the arts, ...n as the Carolingian ...aissance. After he ...erts his subjects to ...stianity the Pope ...ns Charlemagne ...Roman Emperor.

Feudalism in Europe c.800 ...return for land, a peasant works for a Lord, who supports the King during wars.

Raiders from the Sea. 800-950 Starved of land, Vikings set out to seek new territory.

...0 Vikings sight Iceland.
...0 Vikings discover Greenland.
...2 Eric the Red sails to Greenland.

Maori Navigator ...Polynesia, Kupe, ...overs New Zealand.

Bjarni Herjulfsson, ...ndic trader, sights ...n America.

...990 Great Mosque built at ...doba in Spain by Arab ...orish) Conquerors.

...00 The Hopewell ...ans use the etching ...ess.

---

900 Vikings Settle in Normandy, and later they become known as Normans.

962 Emperor of the West. German King, Otto I, who rules the vast Kingdoms of the Germans, parts of France, Italy and lands in central Europe, decides to make himself Holy Roman Emperor and seeks to bring the Pope under his control.

987 Powerful French Lord, Hugh Capet, becomes the first in a long line of kings who rule France for nine centuries.

960 Poland Founded. Prince Miezsko makes Poland into a single state and adopts Christianity.

988 Religion of Russia. Grand Prince Vladimir of Kiev becomes an Orthodox Christian, orders the destruction of non-Christian statues and builds churches in the Byzantine style.

A knight's armour in the Middle Ages

1000s Chinese improve gunpowder so that it can be used for firecrackers and weapons. The chemical mixture used by the Chinese burns rather than explodes.

978 The Chinese begin a massive encyclopedia with 1,000 volumes.

c.1025 Fireplaces with mantels are built in Europe.

c.1026 Musical notes are first named do, re, mi, fa, sol, la by Guido d'Arezzo.

1065 First known stained glass window is placed in Augsburg Cathedral in Germany.

---

c.1000 Indians of North America become efficient farmers. Some live in clusters of houses, called pueblos, with up to 800 rooms.

1014 Battle of Clontarf. Vikings are defeated by Brian Boru in Ireland.

1016 King Canute brings England under his rule.

1066 Battle of Hastings. William of Normandy invades England and kills King Harold. He becomes king.

1086 Domesday Book. This is made for William of Normandy and is a record of people, land and animals in most of England.

The Samurai c.1000 A Japanese warrior class, known as Samurai, becomes important and remains at the centre of Japanese life for several centuries. Samurai follow a code of coduct called bushido and are famed for their loyalty.

1056-1147 Almoravid Kingdom. Almoravids, a Muslim people whose homeland is Morocco, rule a kingdom stretching from Ghana to large parts of southern Spain. They lose their Spanish lands in 1147 to another African tribe, the Almohades.

1000 Leif Ericsson sails from Norway to Greenland. He lands in North America and calls it Vinland.

1030 A medical school is built in Salerno, Italy. European doctors know very little but learn new scientific treatments from Arabian and Jewish doctors who are much more skilled.

c.1100 Very few people can read or write so troubadours, who tell stories in song, are very popular. They tell the tales of King Arthur and his Knights of the Round Table.

1088 The founding of Bologna University leads to a growth in universities. Teachers and students speak and write in Latin, the old Roman language.

English farmers in 1086

1071 Arp Arsian leads a group of Seljuk Turks into battle against the Byzantine Emperor. They win, and establish a large Turkish empire in Armenia. In 1075 they conquer Syria and Palestine.

c.1096 Crusaders Return with many new foods from Arab lands including rice, sugar, lemons and spice. They also bring back beautiful silks and traders start travelling out there to buy these goods.

1050s European workers, such as blacksmiths, weavers and silversmiths, begin to form guilds which protect the workers. The guilds organize training and exams to insure proper learning of skills, and arrange fair pay.

1067 Work begins on sewing the Bayeux Tapestry. It is over seventy metres long and tells the story of the conquest of England by the Normans.

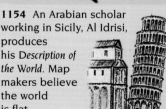

1094 First record of gondolas used, famous boats which are still used today in Venice, Italy.

1100 Inca King. Sinchi Roca becomes first king of the Incas.

The Crusades 1096-1270 Christian Europeans try to regain the holy city of Jerusalem from Muslim rule. Many kings as well as ordinary men set out to fight the Muslims who are holding the city. They believe they are fighting "Holy Wars" and call themselves crusaders. In 1099 they manage to capture Jerusalem but Saladin the Great, a strong Muslim leader, wins it back in 1187. Furthur crusades fail to recapture the city but crusaders bring back new ideas and inventions to Europe.

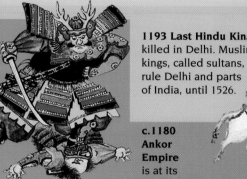

1157-1199 Richard the Lionheart. One of the leaders of the crusades is England's King, Richard I. In his ten year reign he spends only six months at home in England. He is killed besieging a castle in France.

c.1120-1450 Age of Great Zimbabwe, a centre of crafts and industry whose inhabitants work in gold, copper and iron. Modern Zimbabwe is named in its honour.

1154 An Arabian scholar working in Sicily, Al Idrisi, produces his *Description of the World*. Map makers believe the world is flat.

Cathedrals 1100s The great age of cathedral building begins in Europe. Most cathedrals are built in the style called Gothic and take many years to finish. They are the biggest of all Christian churches.

c.1194 Building begins on Chartres Cathedral in France.

c.1163 Building begins on Notre Dame, a famous cathedral in Paris.

1110 First record of firework display in China recorded.

1210 First Christmas carols are written.

The Golden People 1200s The Inca people are very efficient and they make beautiful jewellery and sculpture. From 1400 they begin to rule massive gold-producing territories in South America from their capital in what is now Cuzco.

1215 Magna Carta. Barons rebel against King John and force him to sign Magna Carta. Amongst other things, this document states that the king should obey his own laws.

1209 Franciscans. St Francis of Assisi gives up his rich life to start a new group of monks, the Franciscans. They live in poverty and help the sick. St Francis loves animals.

1212 Children's Crusade. Thousands of children set off to try and fight the holy war. Many die on the way or are sold into slavery.

1193 Last Hindu King killed in Delhi. Muslim kings, called sultans, rule Delhi and parts of India, until 1526.

c.1180 Ankor Empire is at its height in Cambodia.

CENTRAL ASIA

The Great Conqueror 1206-1227 Genghis Khan, whose name means 'very mightly ruler', conquers much of China, Persia, Poland, India and Russia with his people, the Mongols

c.1200 Ethopian Churches. Ten magnificent Christian churches carved from solid rock, are built in Lalibela, the capital of Ethopia.

c.1230 Mali becomes a Muslim kingdom in West Africa. Its capital is Timbuktoo.

c.1200 Arabic numbers, instead of Roman numerals, appear in Europe.

c.1200 In times of peace, knights and noblemen hold tournaments to display their skills in fighting. The early ones are like mock battles and people are often killed, but by this time the tournaments are organized displays of jousting (fighting on horseback with blunt lances).

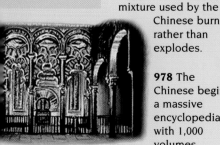

1133 St Bartholomew's Fair starts in London. This is the beginning of great fairs all over Europe, each lasting several weeks. Merchants travel from afar to sell their goods.

1174 Italians start to build the Tower of Pisa, which begins to lean soon afterwards.

1212 Tiles first appear on roofs of London houses instead of thatched and wooden ones.

c.1218 The Danes produce a national flag.

1295 Marco Polo, returning from his great travels, introduces spaghetti to the Italians.

1280 First glass mirror appears.

THE AMERICAS

Aztec c.1300 Mexican Indians settle in Tenochtitlán in 1325 and become very powerful. They worship the sun and perform human sacrifices. They are thought to have killed many people at their religious ceremonies.

c.1400 North America has a population of about one million by now.

Timeline continues on page 24

1381 Peasants' Revolt. As a result of economic disorder and hardship following the Black Death, peasants march to London to confront King Richard II. This uprising is suppressed and its leaders are killed.

EUROPE

1273 Habsburg Dynasty. Rudolf of Habsburg becomes emperor. Habsburgs rule Austria until 1918.

1284 Wales Conquered. Edward I completes his conquest of Wales after the death of Prince Llewelyn.

1314 Battle of Bannockburn. Robert the Bruce wins in battle and strengthens Scotland's claim to independence from English rule.

1327-1377 Edward III is thought by contemporaries to be the perfect chivalrous King, one of the most powerful in Europe. He creates the Order of the Garter, the highest order of Knighthood. He fights many wars abroad, but his reign is a peaceful one in England.

Hundred Years' War 1337-1453 Edward III of England claims the Kingdom of France. Many battles are fought and France eventually wins, with England keeping only Calais and the Channel Islands.

Persecutions of Jews 1182-1290. Jews cannot lead a free life and many massacres take place. France, Portugal, England and Germany, order Jews to leave. Many move east to Poland and Hungary

Black Death Rages 1347. The Black Death, a form of plague thought to have been carried partly by fleas on rats, starts in the East. In 1347 it arrives in Europe in traders' ships. Eventually it kills many people, perhaps one-third of all the people in Europe.

c.1300 Ottoman Empire. Built by Osman I survives until 1923

1260 Kublai Khan, grandson of Genghis Khan, becomes Emperor of China, the first foreigner to rule there.

1358 French Peasants' Protest against high taxes and low wages but their revolt is suppressed.

CHINA

Ming Dynasty 1368 Chu Yuan-Chang, Chinese emperor, drives the Mongols out of China and starts the Ming Dynasty, which lasts until 1644.

1398 Delhi Destroyed by Tamerlane, ruler of Samarkand, in Central Asia.

Tamerlane's Reign of Terror 1369-1405 Tamerlane, descendant of Genghis Khan, conquers huge territories including parts of Russia, Persia, Turkey and India. He defeats Ottoman ruler, Bayazid, in 1402.

c.1200 Ethiopian Churches. Ten magnificent Christian churches carved from solid rock, are built in Lalibela, the capital of Ethiopia.

AFRICA

c.1230 Mali becomes a Muslim Kingdom in West Africa. Its capital is Timbuktoo.

1324 Mansa Musa, King of Mali, goes on a pilgrimage to the holy city of Mecca, the centre of Muslim religion. He is pictured on the *Catalan Atlas*, a map of 1375.

1348-1355 Egypt is devastated by the plague.

1200-1300 In Europe there is no cotton and little silk so most people wear wool clothes. The finest wool comes from England where there are 10 million sheep, and England grows richer as a result. Wool is sold to foreign merchants unwoven. Belgium has the best weavers and Flanders in Belgium is the centre of the weaving trade.

Marco Polo c.1254-1324. Marco Polo is about 15 when he starts a long overland journey travelling from Venice to China. The great Chinese leader Kublai Khan welcomes him and he spends over 20 years living at his court and exploring the Far East.

c.1352 Arab explorer, Ibn Battuta, explores the vast Sahara desert.

Hanseatic League 1356 Northern European ports unite into a league, giving themselves better opportunities for trade. They soon become rich.

c.1250 Italian traders found banks to look after crusaders' money, and start an early system of bank cheques. They also loan money.

1305 King Edward I causes standard measurement, including the foot, yard and acre, to be used in England.

1348 An Italian, Giovanni de Dondi, makes a clock with seven faces which show the movements of the sun, moon and five known planets.

1200s Poems and tales of herioc deeds describe how a true Knight should be not only brave but also a gallant lover and good Christian. This idea is called chivalry, and throughout Europe knights and noblemen try to live up to it.

c.1200 In times of peace, knights and noblemen hold tournaments to display their skills in fighting. The early ones are like mock battles and people are often killed, but by this time the tournaments are organized displays of jousting (fighting on horseback with blunt lances).

Age of Castles 1100-1400. All over Europe, noblemen and their households live in castles, which they use as homes, fortresses, prisons, and bases of local government. Castles can hold out for months if attacked, as long as food and water last. In Germany, at this time, there are over 10,000 castles.

Monks and Monasteries 1000-1400. Monasteries are very important places where groups of monks live and work together. They build many beautiful churches. Monks copy holy books by hand, decorate them beautifully, and are often the only people who can read or write. They also tend the sick, help the poor, teach children and shelter travelers.

1300s In Italy, Dante writes *The Divine Comedy* and Boccaccio *The Decameron* (1350).

c.1289 The Italians first record the use of spectacles.

1340 The Italians construct a paper mill at Fabriano. Seven water-wheels drive the mill.

1309-1354 Alhambra Palace, built by Mohammed in Granada in Muslim Spain, is at its most magnificent at this time.

1320 First known written references to guns.

1300s Chinese people of the Ming Dynasty produce beautiful china and art.

c.1350 The beginning of the legend of Robin Hood.

1370 Steel crossbow first used as a weapon.

1388 Geoffrey Chaucer, an English Knight, writes *The Canterbury Tales*, a group of stories which are among the first to be written in English instead of Latin.

AD250 TO AD1400 ~ MEDIEVAL WAYS OF LIFE

Machu Picchu in Peru, perched high on a mountain shoulder, was a ceremonial city used by Inca lords to worship their gods.

PEOPLES OF THE SUN

The Incas

The Incas held sway over a vast empire which, after 5,000 years of development, was at its height when Pizarro arrived from Spain and captured the Inca king, Atahualpa, in 1532. The empire covered a large area of South America and centred on Cuzco in Peru.

Manco Capaac was the first of 13 Inca emperors. His reign began in about AD1200. The Incas worshipped the sun and their emperors were supposed to be descended directly from the sun god and were worshipped as gods too.

A network of roads ran along the coast and over the Andes mountains - in all about 24,856 miles (40,000 kilometres) of roads. Most of these routes were only a yard wide, just enough for men on foot with llamas for transport. Only official travellers could use the roads.

The Incas were outstanding engineers who made excellent irrigation systems and terraced the hillsides for agriculture. They built suspension bridges over canyons, causeways over marshland, tunnels through mountains and vast storehouses for grain - as well as creating huge fortresses and fine cities.

The Aztecs

• The Aztecs inhabited Mexico from AD1100.

• Their capital, Tenochtitlán, stood on the same site as Mexico City today.

• They were conquered by the Spanish in the early 16th century.

• Their greatest ruler was Montezuma II.

• They made daily sacrifices of human victims to the sun god believing that the end of the world would come otherwise.

• They reclaimed marshland to create some of the finest farming land in the New World.

• Ruled by a priest king, their strong well-equipped army extended their territories.

Known as 'thought paintings' by the Aztecs, this scene from the sacred book, the 'Codex Borbonicus' (Book of Predictions), shows the gods Xiuhtecuhtli and Itztapaltotec.

The Mayas

From 300BC until AD1519 the Maya civilization was at its height. The Mayas were remarkable artists and clever astronomers who made accurate calendars. They lived in Central America, in the Guatemala/Mexico area, creating city states, many of which warred against each other aggressively; enemy captives were likely to become human sacrifices, usually by having their hearts removed.

The Maya invented the first true writing system in pre-Columbian America, with 850 hieroglyphic characters.

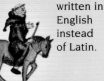

We think of the Vikings as raiders and pirates who set off across the seas to conquer new land, fierce warriors who terrorized those who lived near to the coast and in fear of their approach. So it is hard to believe that they began as peaceful farmers in Scandinavia, growing crops, herding cattle, hunting, fishing and trapping. Gradually these farming settlements spread and as the Scandinavians became traders, dealing in ivory from walrus tusks, in fur and skins, in objects made from silver, wood, amber and soapstone, the need to travel much further afield arose. They had to seek fresh sources of supplies as the demand for goods suddenly increased.

To beat the competition, especially for trade with the Arabs, they began their raids and plunder in fast and shallow longboats that could sail up rivers and move into shores that ordinary boats could not reach. Speed and surprise tactics gave them great advantage over those they attacked.

Raids and settlement

The Vikings were the first people to properly organize communities and trade routes in Russia, between AD882 and 1242. They settled as farmers in places as far as Greenland and Iceland, as well as founding Viking communities in England and Ireland, France and Spain. Monasteries proved an easy target for Viking raids and they plundered many Christian relics. The Vikings were the most powerful force in north-west Europe in the 9th and 10th centuries; they created towns, trade and industry wherever they went.

Their settlement in France was established when Duke Rollo was officially granted land he had seized near the Seine. The Normans evolved from this community.

TOP LEFT: *Vikings were raiders and pirates, but also very good sailors who set off across the seas to conquer new land.*

LEFT: *Illustration of the French castle Mortagne under seige in 1377. The English held out against the French attack for six months.*

CASTLES

Medieval buildings help to give us a picture of how people lived at the time. Although most wooden structures have long since vanished and there are few remains of the more humble homes, many castles have survived. Early castles were towers made of wood, built on a mound (called a motte) and surrounded by a wall, but by the 11th century they were being built of stone, so that they were less vulnerable to attack. Some castles had a drawbridge and moat to make them more secure.

A castle was lived in by a nobleman and his family, but would give protection to people in the surrounding countryside in times of danger.

A FEW FACTS ABOUT CASTLES

• The walls on English castles were usually about 6 - 7 feet (2 metres) thick; in central Europe, fortification walls were much thicker, measuring as much as 65 feet (20 metres); in India and China, medieval forts had walls that ranged from 13 feet (4 metres) up to as much as from 15 to 75 feet (23 metres thick).

• During the 13th century King Edward I of England built a ring of six powerful castles to help enforce his conquest of the Welsh. Caernarvon Castle in North Wales was the most important and remains one of the best preserved in the British Isles.

• The Crusaders built many magnificent castles across Europe and into the East, some of which were seized by the Saracens and helped them to resist the later Crusading armies.

• Round keeps replaced square ones because their strong structure was better able to withstand the on-slaught of weapons such as ballistas and battering rams.

• Some castles, such as The Kremlin in Moscow, were built of brick. Kremlin is the Russian word for citadel.

Maya nobles wearing elaborate headdresses and necklaces, take part in a colourful procession. A fresco from the Temple of Bonampack in Chiapas, Mexico.

AMERICA

The civilizations of the American continent developed later than those of Eurasia and its peoples were ill-prepared for the impact of their European 'discoverers' at the end of the 16th century. Only in Mesoamerica and the Andes were there relatively advanced cultures. The Mayan civilization (in the Yucatan peninsula) collapsed during the 9th century. Northern tribes arrived to establish the Toltec empire in Mexico (in AD 968) but their capital, Tula, was destroyed in 1170. The next new civilization to arise in this area was that of the Aztecs, in the 13th century. Farther south, the territories of the Incas expanded under Pachacuti Inca, who became emperor in 1438. Within 40 years, the Inca Empire stretched 2000 miles along the Andes mountain chain.

CAROLINGIAN EMPIRE

Within a century of the end of the Western Roman Empire, a powerful, unified state was established by the Franks. In 800, their king, Charlemagne, was crowned Emperor of the large area of western Europe which became known as the Holy Roman Empire. After Charlemagne's death, the different parts of the empire began to separate again into what were to become the kingdom of France and, under Otto I, the German empire.

HUNGARY

Eastern Europe remained in turmoil as more tribes moved in from the east, including Turks, Avars, Bulgars and Magyars. They made persistent raids on the west until they were decisively defeated by King Otto I of Germany and began to settle in their own state of Hungary.

In the Toltec/Maya city of Chichén Itzá, Mexico, stands the Temple of the Warriors. The entrance is guarded by a reclining Chacmool figure and by two open-jawed carved stone representations of the god Quetzalcoatl, the Feathered Serpent.

The Byzantine Emperor Justinian I walks to his place of worship with court officials. A 6th century mosaic from the basilica of San Vitale in Ravenna, Italy.

During the reign of Emperor Justinian, Christianity was at the centre of Byzantine affairs. Justinian's greatest architectural achievement is the church of Holy Wisdom, Hagia Sophia, in Constantinople, which was for centuries the most magnificent building in Christendom.

A Muslim merchant mounts his camel for a desert journey, (c.1237). Muslim traders were highly respected members of the community. As a young man, the Prophet Muhammad had been an honest merchant, organising camel caravans which crossed the Arabic desert.

THE VIKINGS

In northern Europe, post-Roman Britain fell prey to invading Angles, Saxons, Danes and Norsemen. In 911, Danish Vikings acquired land in northern France - Normandy - and this powerful new state conquered England in 1066. Norsemen from Scandinavia also moved eastwards. These people, known as Varangians, established a number of principalities in places such as Novogorod and Kiev. These were united at the end of the 10th century to form Rus, an early Russian state. During the 13th century, until their defeat in 1380, the Mongols held sway in this area. They were followed by the state of Muscovy under the leadership of Ivan III, who declared himself in 1480 to be 'Tsar of all the Russias'.

BYZANTIUM

The Byzantine Empire (the Eastern Roman Empire) remained the bastion of European civilization. During the reign of Justinian (527-565), the lands along the Mediterranean coastline were reconquered. By the middle of the 7th century, Islamic Arabs had taken over North Africa and Persia and driven the Byzantines out of Palestine. By the early 8th century they were at the borders of India and had overrun most of Spain, where they were known as 'Moors'.

Christian Europe fought back in the Crusades, which began in 1098, and founded small Christian enclaves in Palestine. Christian kingdoms in northern Spain gradually retook the peninsula and the last Muslim state, Granada, had fallen to them by the end of the 15th century. The vast Islamic empire soon fell apart, although the Seljuk Turks remained powerful and took most of Asia Minor from Byzantium at the Battle of Manzikert in 1071.

THE MONGOL EMPIRE

The Mongols dominated the 13th century, uniting under Genghis Khan (1167-1227). They conquered almost all of Eurasia, including much of Sung dynasty China (in 1234), the Middle East (by 1258), and Kiev in 1240, with a raid that took them to the edge of the German Empire. However, western Europe and Palestine were saved by the timely deaths of the Great Khans in 1241 (Ogedei) and 1259 (Möngke), and the Mongol empire was split into four khanates. Under Kublai Khan (1259-1294) the Mongols completed the conquest of the Chinese Empire where they ruled until 1368. The ferocious adventurer Timur (1336-1405) created an empire in Persia, and his campaigns devasted Delhi, broke the power of the khanate of the Golden Horde and sacked Damascus.

THE OTTOMAN EMPIRE

The Ottoman Turks rose to power in the 14th century. By 1340, they had occupied Thrace, defeated the Serbs at Kosovo in 1389, beaten off a badly organized Crusade in 1396, survived an invasion by Timur in 1402 and finally had taken Constantinople in 1453. The Ottoman Empire would expand and last nearly half a millennium.

EUROPE

The 14th century brought misery to much of Europe. From 1337 to 1453 the Hundred Years' War ravaged large areas of northern and western France, and, between 1347 and 1353 bubonic plague - the Black Death - killed some 20 million people. Christianity survived attack from within and without under the leadership of the papacy, which had gained universal spiritual and legal authority in Europe. During the 15th century, the artistic revolution of the Renaissance in Italy prepared the way for the European domination of the modern world. At the end of the century, Columbus, Cabot and other intrepid sailors ventured beyond the known world, making contact with the civilizations of the New World and ushering in a new phase of history.

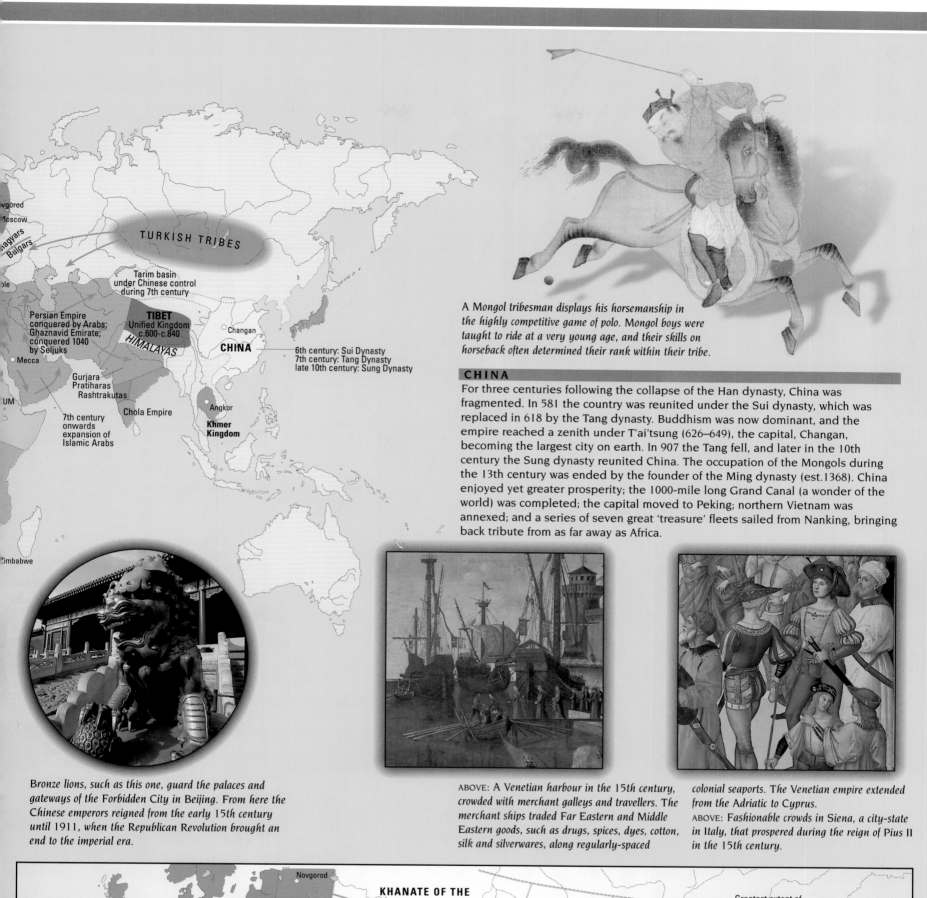

TURKISH TRIBES

Tarim basin
under Chinese control
during 7th century

TIBET
Unified Kingdom
c.600–c.840

Persian Empire
conquered by Arabs;
Ghaznavid Emirate;
conquered 1040
by Seljuks

HIMALAYAS

Changan

CHINA

6th century: Sui Dynasty
7th century: Tang Dynasty
late 10th century: Sung Dynasty

Mecca

Gurjara
Pratiharas
Rashtrakutas

7th century
onwards
expansion of
Islamic Arabs

Chola Empire

Angkor

Khmer
Kingdom

A Mongol tribesman displays his horsemanship in
the highly competitive game of polo. Mongol boys were
taught to ride at a very young age, and their skills on
horseback often determined their rank within their tribe.

CHINA

For three centuries following the collapse of the Han dynasty, China was
fragmented. In 581 the country was reunited under the Sui dynasty, which was
replaced in 618 by the Tang dynasty. Buddhism was now dominant, and the
empire reached a zenith under T'ai'tsung (626–649), the capital, Changan,
becoming the largest city on earth. In 907 the Tang fell, and later in the 10th
century the Sung dynasty reunited China. The occupation of the Mongols during
the 13th century was ended by the founder of the Ming dynasty (est.1368). China
enjoyed yet greater prosperity; the 1000-mile long Grand Canal (a wonder of the
world) was completed; the capital moved to Peking; northern Vietnam was
annexed; and a series of seven great 'treasure' fleets sailed from Nanking, bringing
back tribute from as far away as Africa.

Bronze lions, such as this one, guard the palaces and
gateways of the Forbidden City in Beijing. From here the
Chinese emperors reigned from the early 15th century
until 1911, when the Republican Revolution brought an
end to the imperial era.

ABOVE: A Venetian harbour in the 15th century,
crowded with merchant galleys and travellers. The
merchant ships traded Far Eastern and Middle
Eastern goods, such as drugs, spices, dyes, cotton,
silk and silverwares, along regularly-spaced

colonial seaports. The Venetian empire extended
from the Adriatic to Cyprus.
ABOVE: Fashionable crowds in Siena, a city-state
in Italy, that prospered during the reign of Pius II
in the 15th century.

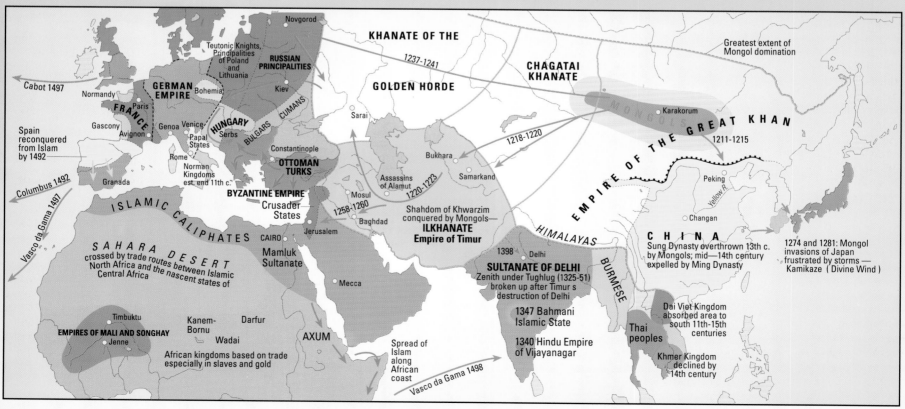

Novgorod

KHANATE OF THE

Greatest extent of
Mongol domination

Cabot 1497

Teutonic Knights,
Principalities
of Poland
and
Lithuania

RUSSIAN
PRINCIPALITIES

GOLDEN HORDE

1237-1241

CHAGATAI
KHANATE

GERMAN
EMPIRE

Bohemia

Kiev

Normandy

FRANCE

Paris

Karakorum

Spain
reconquered
from Islam
by 1492

Gascony

Avignon

Genoa

Venice

HUNGARY
Serbs

CUMANS

Sarai

MONGOLS

EMPIRE OF THE GREAT KHAN

1211-1215

Columbus 1492

Rome

Papal
States

BULGARS

1218-1220

Bukhara

Samarkand

Peking

Granada

Norman
Kingdoms
est. end 11th c.

Constantinople

OTTOMAN
TURKS

BYZANTINE EMPIRE
Crusader
States

Assassins
of Alamut

1220-1223

Changan

Yellow R.

Vasco da Gama 1497

ISLAMIC CALIPHATES

Mosul

1258-1260

Baghdad

Shahdom of Khwarzim
conquered by Mongols—

ILKHANATE
Empire of Timur

HIMALAYAS

CHINA
Sung Dynasty overthrown 13th c.
by Mongols; mid—14th century
expelled by Ming Dynasty

1274 and 1281: Mongol
invasions of Japan
frustrated by storms —
Kamikaze (Divine Wind)

SAHARA DESERT
crossed by trade routes between Islamic
North Africa and the nascent states of
Central Africa

CAIRO

Jerusalem

Mamluk
Sultanate

1398

Delhi

SULTANATE OF DELHI
Zenith under Tughlug (1325-51)
broken up after Timur's
destruction of Delhi

BURMESE

Dai Viet Kingdom
absorbed area to
south 11th-15th
centuries

Mecca

1347 Bahmani
Islamic State

Thai
peoples

Timbuktu

Kanem-
Bornu

Darfur

Wadai

AXUM

EMPIRES OF MALI AND SONGHAY

Jenne

African kingdoms based on trade
especially in slaves and gold

Spread of
Islam
along
African
coast

1340 Hindu Empire
of Vijayanagar

Khmer Kingdom
declined by
14th century

Vasco da Gama 1498

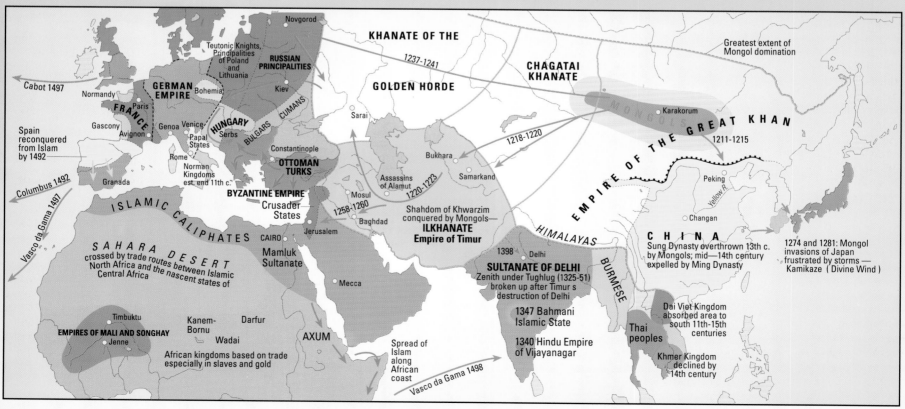

THE AMERICAS

EUROPE

1400 Welshman Owen Glendower Rebels against England and proclaims himself Prince of Wales, but his army is defeated.

1431 France. It is said that Joan of Arc is burnt as a witch after leading the French army to end the siege of Orléans.

1439 Russian Orthodox Church separates from the Greek church.

CHINA

1405-1433 Chinese explorer Cheng Ho makes seven voyages to India, Persia and Africa. China begins to trade with all these countries. Under the Ming Dynasty, China expands, invades Mongolia and Vietnam and sends diplomats around the world.

Christopher Columbus 1451-1506 While other explorers look for eastward sea routes to India, Italian sailor Columbus tries sailing westwards instead. He lands on the Caribbean islands in 1492, thinks that they are India, and calls them the West Indies.

1450s German goldsmith Johann Gutenburg invents a moveable type which can be used again and again to print different books. Within 50 years printing presses have been set up in over 200 places in Europe. Many more people learn to read and write and the ideas of renaissance and the reformation spread quickly.

1403 Chinese scholar Yung Lo compiles a huge encyclopedia in 22,937 volumes. Only three copies are made.

c.1410 Russian Andrei Rublev is the greatest painter of pictures of saints called icons.

1450-1518 Dutch artist Hieronymous Bosch paints religious pictures filled with monsters.

1493 Christopher Columbus. Following the expeditions of Christopher Columbus, the Spanish make their first New World settlement on the island of Hispaniola.

1455-1485 Wars of the Roses. The Dukes of Lancaster and York quarrel about who should be King of England and their armies fight a long war. Yorkists use a white rose as their symbol whilst Lancastrians use a red one. The wars ends when Lancastrian Henry beats King Richard III in battle and becomes the first Tudor King, Henry VII.

1513 Scotland. English and Scottish armies fight at the battle of Flodden. King James IV of Scotland is killed.

1520 Flanders. Henry VIII of England and Francis I of France meet at the Field of the Cloth of Gold to make peace between their countries.

MIDDLE EAST

1453 Constantinople is captured when Ottomans overthrow the Byzantine Empire renaming it Istanbul. Many historians see this date as the end of the Middle Ages. The Turks become leaders of the Muslim world and destroy many Christian states, taking control of parts of North Africa and other countries around Eastern Mediterranean.

ASIA

1467-1568 Japan. Local barons called daimyos fight against each other in a series of civil wars lasting more than 100 years.

1464 Songhai Empire. Sunni Ali becomes ruler of the Songai people in West Africa. They trade across the Sahara desert and live on the river Niger. In 1468 they capture Timbuktoo and over the next 80 years they destroy the Mali Empire.

1471-1574 Portuguese Expeditions settle on many parts of the African coast from Tunis in the North to Angola and Mozambique in the south.

1488 Portuguese sailor, Bartholomeu Dias, reaches the Cape of Good Hope, the southern tip of Africa, looking for a way to sail to India and the Spice Islands, and Prince Henry of Portugal, known as the Navigator, sets up a school of navigation.

1497-1498 Vasco da Gama sails from Portugal to India.

1513 Spanish explorer Balboa is the first European to reach the Pacific coast of America by travelling overland.

Renaissance Beginning in the 1400s, the Italian Renaissance, or "rebirth", is an age of fresh interest in the art and the learning of the ancient Greeks and Romans. Painters, scientists, musicians, sculptors and architects flourish in Italian cities with help from rich noblemen. Famous artists include Botticelli, Leonardo da Vinci, Michaelangelo and Raphael. People aim to become well-educated in many subjects and new ideas spread quickly across Europe.

1450 The first brandy is made in Modena, Italy.

1507 Europeans Name the New World America, after Italian explorer Amerigo Vespucci.

1509-1547 Henry VIII, son of Henry VII, rules England. He wants a son to follow him as King, so he seeks a divorce from his wife, Catherine, who only has one daughter. When the Pope refuses, because he is influenced by his enemies, Henry breaks with the Roman Church and makes himself head of the Church of England. He closes down the monasteries and takes their land and treasure. He marries six times, and has two of his wives beheaded for treason.

1513 Scotland. English and Scottish armies fight at the Battle of Flodden. King James IV of Scotland is killed.

1520 Flanders. Henry VIII of England and Francis I of France meet at the field of the Cloth of Gold to make peace between their countries.

1520 Suleiman I rules the Ottoman Empire for 46 years. Europeans name him the Magnificent, but the Turks call him Kanuni, lawgiver, because of reforms in law and government. He develops the Ottoman navy into a powerful force.

c.1500 China. Mongols and Japanese attack China.

1510 African Slaves are taken across the Atlantic Ocean to work in sugar plantations.

1517 Ottoman Turks conquer Egypt, and gradually push their way into Ethiopia and Tunisia.

1519 Ferdinand Magellan leaves from Spain with five ships to sail round the world. He finds a sea route around South America into the Pacific Ocean. Magellan is killed in the Philippines, but the expedition completes the amazing voyage.

Leonardo da Vinci 1452-1519 is a Renaissance painter most famous for pictures such as the Mona Lisa. He is also an architect, engineer and inventor, and he studies music and science.

1465 First printed music appears in Europe.
c.1489 The + (plus) and - (minus) signs first come into use for mathematicians.

1534 French Explorers led by Jacques Cartier are the first Europeans to reach Canada.

1537-1600 South America. The Spanish and Portuguese set up colonies in many places on the continent of South America.

1542 Charles V, King of Spain, passes new laws forbidding slavery in the Spanish colonies.

1519-1521 Mexico. Hernan Cortes, a Spanish conquistador, leads a small army of 550 men into the land of the Aztecs. It takes them only two years to win control of the whole Empire.

Charles V (r.1516-1556) the King of Spain and Holy Roman Emperor, is the most powerful man in Europe. He stops the Turkish advance into Western Europe and encourages exploration in the Americas, winning great riches and prestige for Spain. He retires from the throne in 1556 and leaves Spain to his son, Philip, and the Empire to his brother Ferdinand.

1547 Ivan the Terrible calls himself Tsar or emperor. He conquers many terrritories, including Siberia. After Poland defeats his army he begins a reign of terror, and his secret police murder many people. By the time Ivan dies in 1584, he is insane.

INDIA   1526 India. Babur, a descendant of Tamerlane, enters India from Afghanistan and defeats the Sultan of Delhi. He is the first of the Muslim Mogul rulers of India.

1543 Nicholaus Copernicus, a Polish priest, develops a theory that the earth and other planets orbit around the sun. Most people of his time believe that the sun goes around the earth.

1543 Flemish doctor, Andreas Vesalius, publishes *De Humani Corporis Fabrica,* the first book to contain accurate pictures of human anatomy drawn from life.

The Inquisition 1478 used by the monarchy in Spain to deal with political and religious opponents. About 200,000 Jews are forced to leave the country, together with Arabs and Christian heretics.

c.1517 Coffee made from South American beans is drunk in Europe for the first time. Explorers bring back tobacco, chocolate and turkeys.

1532-1572 Peru. Francisco Pizarro, another conquistador, reaches Peru. The Spaniards their horses and canons easily defeat the In They steal much Inca treasure and force the people to work in silver mines, where many The last Inca ruler, Tupac Amaru, is captured in

1554 Mary I (r.1553-1558), elder daughter Henry VIII, marries Philip II of Spain and ma England Catholic again. During her reign m Protestants are persecuted and some, mart

Elizabeth I, Henry VIII's second daughter, reigns for 45 years (1558-1603). She brings back Protestantism as state religion and puts an end to Catholic plots encouraged by Mary, Queen of Scots, by ordering her execution. She encourages trade and exploration, especially in the Americas, and is a clever diplomat. She never marries. The "Elizabethan Age" is famous literature, music and architecture.

1562-1598 France. Religious wars betwee Catholics and Protestants lead to man deaths on both sides, in incidents such St Bartholomew's Day Massacre. In 1 the Edict of Nantes finally gives Prote and Catholics equal political rights.

1568-1648 Dutch Revolt. The people the Netherlands rebel against the Sp in order to gain th independence. Th fighting ends in freedom for the se Northern Province ruled by the royal House of Orange.

1542 Mary Stuart becomes Queen of Scotland when she is only one week old. Five years later, she is sent to France and lives at the French court.

1556-1605 Akbar the Great rules India. He tries to unite the country by allowing Hindus to practise their religion, and extends Mogul rule eastwards to Bengal and westwards to Sind. He builds many beautiful palaces

1569 Dutch ma maker Mercato draws a new k of map for sa which shows

1469-1527 Italian statesman Niccolo Machiavelli writes famous guide to using politi power.

Reformation 1500s Martin Luther, a German priest, pin list of 95 theses or protests t church door in Wittenburg a starts the reform of the Cath church. In 1521 the Diet of Worms (a council held in the city of Worms) outlaws Luther, but he sets up his own organiza of Protestant Christ in Germany. Swiss Protestant, John Cal spreads his ideas i Scotland, France an the Netherlands. Th Catholic Church trie win people back in movement called th Counter-Reformati

1540s French surgeon Am Paré fits mechanical artifi limbs to wounded soldier

7 North America. The English government s Humphrey Gilbert permission to make ements in North America. He establishes the English colony in Newfoundland in 1583.

579 Francis Drake, sailor and adventurer, aims New Albion (California) for the English uring his voyage around the world.

584 Walter Raleigh, an Englishman, starts a olony in Virginia.

3 nish ada. p II ns the ish ne and s a of mous hips 10,000 rs and 20,000 soldiers. Chased by smaller, er English ships armed with powerful cannons, Armada is wrecked by violent storms. Only a Spanish ships manage to return to Spain.

St Bartholomew's Day Massacre

71 Battle of Lepanto. Off the coast of eece, a huge fleet assembled by the Pope d led by Don John of Austria feats an even bigger toman fleet. This ds the Turkish reat to rope m the sea.

7-1629 Persia. Shah Abbas the Great rules sia. He brings peace and hires two Englishmen ain his armies in European fighting methods.

2 Japan. Hideyoshi, a great military leader who born a peasant, becomes a High Councillor. He ceeds in bringing peace to the country.

8 Ahmed al Mansur, ruler of Fez, leads the roccans. They move into the Sahara and defeat Songhai at the Battle of Tondibi in 1591.

es of the earth as ght lines. Mercator's m is still used for s today.

1596-1597 Dutch explorer William Barents, looking for a way to reach East Asia, sails to the Arctic Ocean north of Russia.

1590s Dutch spectacle-maker, Zacharias Janssen, invents the microscope, a scientific instrument using a number of lenses to make small objects look bigger.

liam Shakespeare **4-1616** One of greatest matists in the ld, he begins his king life as an or. He writes many ys of different ds, histories, edies and edies.

s Metal nuts and are used in Europe ten things together. **5** The first pencil a graphite lead and den cover is ned in Switzerland. The Gregorian dar, which is still throughout the today, first comes se.

c.1586 The first Kabuki play is performed in Japan. It is intended for ordinary people to watch, and not just the rich.

c.1589 The first "water closet", or toilet, comes into use in England. It has a flushing cistern and drains into an underground sewage tank.

c.1589 The first knitting machine is invented in England.

Native Americans

1597 Ireland. Hugh O'Neill, Earl of Tyrone, leads a war against the English Crown which ends with the Treaty of Melifont.

1603 Great Elizabethan Age ends with the death of Elizabeth I.

1605 Gunpowder Plot. Catholics conspire to blow up Protestant King and Parliament. Guy Fawkes, with seven conspirators, is arrested and executed. "Guy Fawkes Day" is still celebrated in England with bonfires and fireworks.

Ottoman Empire 1600-1699. Ottoman Turks attack Central Europe and occupy huge areas there, in the Middle East and North Africa. But their Empire becomes too large to control.

1603-1868 Shogun Era. Tokugawa Iyeyasu seizes power in 1603 and starts shogunate (military dictatorship) lasting until 1868. He persecutes Christian missionaries and

1600's Oyo Kingdom in Nigeria, at the height of its power, produces beautiful bronzes.

1626 Madagascar. First French traders settle on this large island off the east coast of Africa.

1600s Australia. Dutch sailors, blown west from the tip of South Africa, discover Australia by accident.

1602-1603 North America. Spanish explore coast of California.

1606 Pacific Ocean. Spanish discover Tahiti.

1607-1610 Canada. English navigator, Henry Hudson, sails through Hudson strait to southern-most part of Hudson Bay and thinks he is in the Pacific Ocean. His crew mutiny and cast him away to die.

1616 South America. Dutch explorer, Willem Schouten, sails round Cape Horn, the extreme tip of South America.

1616-1618 South America. Sir Walter Raleigh, English explorer and writer, is released from the Tower of London to search for South American gold. He fails.

1609 German astronomer, Johan Kepler, publishes laws about the movement of planets.

1628 English scientist, William Harvey, shows that blood is pumped around the body by the heart.

1609 Thomas Ravenscroft, Englishman, writes *Three Blind Mice*.

1600s Belief in witchcraft grows in Europe.

1611 James I's Authorized English language version of the Bible is published. It is still used today.

1612 Biggest Christian church in the world, the basilica of St. Peter's in Rome, is completed.

1605 Cervantes, a Spaniard, writes *Don Quixote*, the first proper novel.

1607 First forks are used in Italy (knives and spoons are much older).

1619 Slaves First Brought to Virginia from West Africa.

1620 The Pilgrim Fathers. 102 men, women and children, seeking new life and freedom to worship God as they think right, set sail from England in the *Mayflower*. After a dangerous, stormy voyage, they land at Plymouth Rock, Massachusetts, and start a colony.

The Thirty Years' War 1618-1648 Terrible series of wars in Europe starts with a religious dispute in Bohemia. One remarkable event in the early part of the conflict is the Defenestration of Prague, when two administrators are thrown out of a window. War ends with the treaty of Westphalia

1611-1632 Great Swedish King and brilliant general, Gustavus Adolphus, wages war with Denmark, Russia and Poland. He is killed while leading his army at the Battle of Lutzen in Germany.

German Foot soldier

The Ottoman Empire

drives out European traders, ending great period of Portugese trading.

CHINA

1644 Manchus Overthrow Ming dynasty and establish their own Ch'ing dynasty lasting nearly 300 years. During this period many Europeans visit China, buying silks, tea and pottery in exchange for gold and silver. Chinese call the Europeans "barbarians".

1637 Japanese People forbidden to travel abroad.

1674-1681 China. Governors of southern and western provinces rebel unsuccessfully against Manchu control.

1625 Africa. French establish trading post at Cayenne, Guyana.

1626 North America. Dutch found New Amsterdam, now known as New York.

Abel Tasman

1642-1644 Australia. Dutch navigator, Abel Tasman, sails right around Australia without realizing it is there and lands on Diemen's Land, later called Tasmania after him. He also discovers New Zealand but thinks it is part of a huge land mass.

1630 West Indies. Pirates, known as buccaneers, settle in Tortuga.

1637 Pacific Ocean. Russian explorers cross land mass of Siberia and reach the Pacific.

Sir Walter Raleigh

1643 Italian, Evangelista Torricelli, invents the barometer.

1649-1660 The Commonwealth. England now becomes a Commonwealth under powerful and puritanical Oliver Cromwell. Dancing, horse-racing and Sunday sports are forbidden under his rule. In 1653 Cromwell is made "Lord Protector", after refusing the title of King.

Gustavus Adolphus

English Civil War 1642-1646 King Charles I quarrels with Parliament over taxes, religion and royal power and rules without a government from 1629 to 1640, a period called the Eleven Years' Tyranny. This leads to a civil war fought between supporters of the King, the Cavaliers, and the Protestant Parliamentarians, the Roundheads, who fight in Oliver Cromwell's New Model Army. Charles I is finally defeated in 1647 and executed in 1649.

Galileo Galilei 1642. This brilliant Italian mathematician, astronomer and physicist, discovers how the pendulum works. He makes a telescope through which he discovers Jupiter's satellites and the sunspots and he sees the mountains and craters on the moon. He finds that Copernicus is correct in observing that the earth circles the sun, but Galileo is persecuted by the Catholic church for saying so.

1632-1653 20,000 men labour for 20 years in India to build Taj Mahal, a tomb for Shah Jahan's favourite wife.

1637 Founder of modern philosophy, René Descartes, proclaims, "I think, therefore I am."

Baroque Imagination 1600s Very ornate style with many swirls and twirls develops as Italians grow tired of classical ideals.

1608 First telescope is invented by Dutchman Hans Lippershey.

1620 First record of a merry-go-round, in Turkey.

1621 Fairy tale is printed in England for first time: *The History of Tomb Thumb the Little*.

1623 William Shakespeare's plays are published for the first time in book form, called *First Folios*.

1624 First working submarine is built.

1635 First printing press in America is set up in Massachusetts.

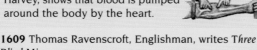

Settlement of North America 1600s.
Explorers and traders colonize parts of North America and Canada. The English set up 13 colonies on the East coast.

— 1680 New Hampshire
— 1629 Massachusetts
— 1664 New York
— 1635 Rhode Island
— 1636 Connecticut
— 1681 Pennsylvania
— 1664 New Jersey
— 1632 Maryland
— 1702 Delaware   1653 NEW AMSTERDAM
— 1607 Virginia
— 1607 North Carolina
— 1670 South Carolina
— 1732 Georgia

THE AMERICAS
1683 Quaker beginnings. Englishman, William Penn, founds Pennsylvania and its Quaker colony.

1692 Salem Witchcraft Trials in New England. Many are accused of witchcraft. Nineteen people are executed, and 150 are imprisoned.

Timeline continues on page 30

1660 The Restoration. The English Republic ends as Charles II becomes King.
1665 London Tragedy. The Great Plague, a disease probably carried by fleas on rats, breaks out in many parts of Europe, killing 68,000 people in London alone.

EUROPE

1666 Great Fire of London starts in king's bakers in Pudding Lane. Fire tears through London, destroying St. Paul's Cathedral as well as 84 churches.

1688 The Glorious Revolution. Catholic James II annoys Parliament by taking too much power; he loses his throne. Protestant Dutch ruler, William of Orange, married to James' daughter, Mary, becomes King. British kings and queens now have less power

Sun King 1638-1715. Louis XIV is King of France for 72 years. The reign of this extraordinary king produces a golden age of art and literature.

1652-1674 The Anglo-Dutch Wars. English and Dutch navies clash when a Dutch fleet in English waters refuses to salute the English flag. The countries are jealous of each other's trading success. Weakened by many land wars against France (1672-1713), Holland loses some of her power, but this tiny country still remains the greatest trading nation in the world.

INDIA Mogul Empire Emperor Shah Jahan (r.1627-1658) extends conquest of India begun by Akbar the Great. Mogul Aurangzeb (r.1658-1707) kills his brothers, imprisons his father and seizes power. He continues conquest of India, and adds Pakistan and part of Afghanistan to his empire. Revolts finally lead to the Empire's decline.
1676 Sikhs Rise against Aurangzeb.

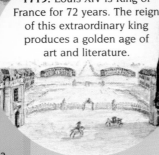

1689 Peter the Great (r.1682-1725) seizes total power in Russia and begins a period of modernization and expansion. In 1695 he makes secret visits to Western Europe, in search of ideas to modernize Russia.

1652 South Africa. Dutchman, Jan van Riebeck, first explorer of southern Africa, meets the Hottentots near Table Bay.

AFRICA 1662 Kongo Kingdom is destroyed by the Portuguese.

1672 Slave Trade in West Africa increases.

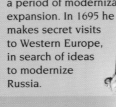
Africa 1660

Morocco Egypt
Timbuktoo Benin Kongo

East India Companies 1600s
English, Dutch, French and Danish companies begin to trade in the East Indies, the "Spice Islands" (Indonesia), and some do business in the Americas and India as well. Trade brings wealth and power to England, Holland and France, but also causes jealousy and war on land and at sea.

Golden Age of Dutch Painting 1600s
Holland produces not only great seafarers, traders and scientists, but also great painters: Rembrandt, Vermeer, Steen and Hals.

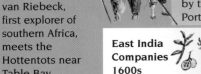

1682 North America. La Salle claims the Mississippi and it's valley for France, naming the region Lousiana in honour of Louis XIV.

1642-1727 English Scientist, Isaac Newton, invents the reflective telescope and shows that white light is really a mixture of colours. Seeing an apple falling from a tree he asks the question "Why do things fall?" In answer, he develops the law of gravitation.

1682 Edmund Halley, English astronomer, first observes the comet now named "Halley's Comet".

1663 Danish physician, Nicolaus Steno, shows that the heart is actually a muscle.

1652 Japanese are the first people to blow their noses with paper tissues.
1656 Dutchman, Christian Huygens, makes the first pendulum clock.
1658 Dutch biologist, Jan Swammerdam, first sees the red cells of blood.
1654 First sugar plantation is established in West Indies.

1661-1708, 30,000 workers build Louis XIV's magnificent Palace of Versailles, one of the most extravagant buildings in the world. French nobility lead idle lives at Versailles and sow seeds of discontent leading to the French revolution a century later.
1670 First minute hands are put on watches.
1675 Speed of light first calculated by a Dane, Olaus Roemer.
1662 Punch and Judy show is first presented in London.

1669 Fierce Mogul Emperor, Aurangzeb, bans Hindu religion in India.
1670 Frenchman, La Fontaine, publishes his Fables.
1675-1710 St Paul's Cathedral is rebuilt after Great Fire. Masterpiece of Sir Christopher Wren, one of the most famous English architects.

1680 The Dodo becomes extinct.

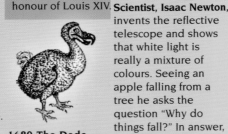

1685 Louis XIV bans all religions except Catholicism in France, causing half a million Huguenots (Protestants) to flee the country

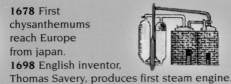

1678 First chysanthemums reach Europe from Japan.
1698 English inventor, Thomas Savery, produces first steam engine.

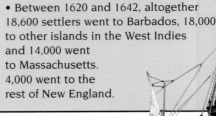

AD1400 TO AD1800 ~ CULTURE, PILGRIMS...

THE RENAISSANCE

MICHELANGELO   DANTE

Renaissance is a term that describes the cultural achievements that began in Italy in the 14th century. The term renaissance means 'rebirth' and refers to a revival in the values and the styles of art, architecture and literature of Ancient Greece and Rome. Scholars and artists applied to their works classical ideas which emphasized that human life was as important as any of the religious subjects favoured at the time.

In literature, Dante (1265-1321), Petrarch (1304-74) and Boccaccio (1313-75), began to explore human nature. In art, landscape and the human form began to be presented more realistically in the works of Giotto (1267-1337), Masaccio (1401-28) and Botticelli (1445-1510) and the sculptures of Donatello (1386-1466). This reached its greatest artistic representation in masterpieces by Leonardo da Vinci (1452-1519), Michelangelo (1475-1564) and Raphael (1483-1520). In architecture, Brunelleschi (1377-1446), Alberti (1404-72), Bramante (c1444-1514) and Palladio (1505-80), created buildings that could compare with the best in the ancient world. During the Renaissance, there was a great interest in many fields of study, including science and technology.

Rich noble families, such as the Medicis of Florence, the d'Estes of Ferrara, the Viscontis and Sforzas of Milan, the Gonzagas of Mantua and the popes, Julius II and Leo X, in Rome, were patrons to many great artists and commissioned works to enhance the reputation of their city-states, celebrate their standing in society and immortalize their names.

> **Did you know that...**
> • **The Pilgrim Fathers** were not actually called The Pilgrim Fathers until 200 years after they had arrived in New England. They were called the 'Old Comers' and the 'Forefathers'.
> • In 1620, 102 settlers seeking greater religious freedom set off from Plymouth, England in their ship, the *Mayflower*. They landed in Massachusetts after a long and dangerous voyage. There were fierce storms and one of the main beams cracked but, after 66 days, the ship arrived safely, having lost just one servant boy and one sailor. That first winter was very severe and nearly half the colony died. However, those who survived gradually became used to their new country and soon more settlers followed - to form other colonies along the coast.
> • The *Mayflower* set sail three times! She left first from Southampton with another ship, the *Speedwell*, but was forced to return because the *Speedwell* was leaking. They set off again from Dartmouth but still the *Speedwell* leaked. So finally the *Mayflower* set off alone, this time from Plymouth.
> • A baby boy born during the voyage was named Oceanus.
> • Between 1620 and 1642, altogether 18,600 settlers went to Barbados, 18,000 to other islands in the West Indies and 14,000 went to Massachusetts. 4,000 went to the rest of New England.

The Mayflower was originally a cargo ship, and not designed to carry passengers.

> **Did you know that...**
> • Condemned witches were often burned at the stake because fire was supposed to drive out any demons.
> • Witches were supposed to walk backwards and be unable to cry

PLAGUE, KINGS AND WITCHES

TOP: *The Great Fire of London, 1666. Despite the destruction of tens of thousands of buildings, London continued to house more than one in ten of the country's population.* ABOVE: *Lemonnier's painting of Louis XIV unveiling a new statue at Versailles.*

LOUIS XIV, THE SUN KING (1638-1715)

Louise XIV was one of the most flamboyant French kings. He inherited the throne as a child of four, too young to rule immediately, but he insisted on taking control of state affairs at the age of sixteen and created an 'absolute monarchy': the king ruled overall. Because he was a strong, dominant character he could manage this very well. His successors did rather less well and this helped to bring about the French Revolution.

Louis' court was rich and extravagant. There were ballets, plays, masques and operas, fêtes and hunting excursions. Louis sought glory through magnificence: by encouraging literature and the arts; through fine palaces with wonderful gardens such as Versailles; through many admiring mistresses; and through constant wars with other countries. He began his day eating breakfast on a service of porcelain and gold and a procession of ten presented his dinner at one o'clock.

WITCHCRAFT

A belief in witches and devils has been around for a long time. They were depicted in prehistoric caves, mentioned in the Bible and described by Homer in ancient Greece. They appear in the folklore of many countries - in Africa, New Zealand and in Guatemala - as well as in Europe.

It was in medieval times, however, that superstition and the belief in witches was at its height and the persecution of those suspected of being 'in league with the devil' led to enormous cruelty.

Witch trials began in earnest in the 12th century and by the time of the Inquisition in the next century many women - and some men too - were accused of evil acts. A good number of these so-called witches were probably just old women who were becoming senile or eccentric and other victims were often accused for reasons of fear or revenge or even greed.

It is interesting that when new laws were passed in Spain in 1610, saying that the property of those convicted could not be confiscated - so there were no

longer any 'goodies' to be seized - the numbers of those accused dropped dramatically.

Matthew Hopkins, Witchfinder General from 1644, travelled through England charging a fee for the discovery of witches. He was responsible for causing a great deal of suffering and many dreadful trials and executions, and was eventually accused of witchcraft himself and hanged in 1647.

Many victims confessed to being witches under torture. They were blamed for disease and famine, unexpected deaths, still-born babies, problems with crops or cattle or sheep and even frost in the vineyards. Many cats were killed too at this time, as, together with toads, they were believed to be witches, 'familiars' or demons.

The Witch Trials at Salem

When the English settlers went to America they took their belief in witches with them.

In 1692 a group of teenage girls began a series of accusations against others in their settlement of Salem in Massachusetts. This developed into a long,

THE FIRE OF LONDON

The fire began in a baker's shop in Pudding Lane. It raged for four days from 2nd-5th September 1666 and burned all of the city except the north-eastern and far western areas. Eighty-seven parish churches and about 13,200 houses were destroyed in the fire. Even wharves and shipping burned. The blaze may have helped bring an end to the ravages of the Great Plague.

Sir Christopher Wren was one of a team of people who supervised the rebuilding of the city: his greatest achievement was the new St Paul's Cathedral.

PLAGUE

History tells of many plagues, spread mainly by rats or mice and fleas. Sweeping through human populations in waves, plague brought rapid death to many. In the 14th century the Black Death killed almost three quarters of the population in parts of Europe; overall about one quarter of the population died, about 25,000,000 people, not to mention those in central Asia, India and China.

'Bring out your dead!' went up the cry when the Great Plague arrived in London in 1664. Carried by rats, mice and fleas, it spread across England but was fiercest in the overcrowded capital. Plague comes in three main forms: bubonic plague which causes great dark swellings, pneumonic plague which affects the lungs and another kind which poisons the blood. Death comes very quickly. Plague kept breaking out in Europe but London escaped until Autumn 1664, when at first just a handful of people died. By the following May the disease was spreading and at the end of that year the Great Plague had arrived in force. Nearly 70,000 deaths had been recorded and there were probably far more than that. About 6,400 people were said to have died of 'spotted fever' which is likely to have been another form of the plague.

Further outbreaks took many lives in other countries, including North Africa, Austria, Germany, Hungary, Poland, and Turkey:

- **1666-70** Bad outbreak
- **1667-69** Outbreaks in the Netherlands
- **1675** Malta 11,000 deaths
- **1679** Vienna 76,000 deaths
- **1681** Prague 83,000 deaths
- **1682** Halle, Germany 4,397 deaths in a population of only 10,000
- **1720** Marseilles 40,000 died in the city; 10,000 in the countryside nearby

---

Did you know that...
- In all, 800,000 people died in Britain as a result of the Black Death between the years 1347 and 1350.

- Despite the enormous damage to buildings, only eight people died as a result of the Fire of London.

- By September 1665, when the Great Plague in London was at its height, over a thousand corpses a day were being put into the communal graves.

---

drawn-out trial. More than thirty people were convicted, many were executed and one man was pressed to death between weighted planks when he refused to plead either guilty or not guilty.

This event is vividly depicted in the play, *The Crucible*, by American writer Arthur Miller.

EUROPE

1707 England and Scotland join to form Great Britain, with one parliament representing the people of two countries.

1714 Death of Queen Anne. None of her 17 children survive her. A distant German cousin who speaks no English becomes King George I.

1715 and 1745 Jacobite Rebellions. Scottish people support the exiled descendants of James II, James Stuart and his son, Charles Edward, known as "Bonny Prince Charlie". They rebel against George I but are defeated by English troops at Culloden. Many are executed. Charles Edward escapes to France.

1701-1713 War of Spanish Succession. When King Charles II of Spain dies childless, many countries in Europe fight to decide who should succeed to the throne of such a rich country. Most battles take place in Italy, Germany and the Netherlands. Eventually, a French prince becomes King Philip V of Spain.

MIDDLE EAST

INDIA

1725-1774 Robert Clive, sent to India as a young man to work for the East India Trading Company, emerges as a brilliant soldier. He wins a series of battles against Indian rulers and against the French. At the age of 33 he is virtual ruler, on behalf of the Company, of vast areas of East India. His conquests lead to enormous wealth for the Company, as well as new trade opportunities.

1700 Bantu Kingdom of Buganba develops in East Africa and Asante power expands on the west coast.

1747-1748 Yoruba People conquer Dahomey and Benin.

1716 Emperor Ch'ien Lung bans Christianity in China.

1719 Daniel Defoe, an Englishman, writes *Robinson Crusoe,* based on the true story of a shipwreck.

The Age of Reason: the Enlightenment

1650-1750 Philosophers such as Voltaire, Rousseau and Thomas Paine argue that society should be organized according to rules based not on religion but on reason, or rational thought. The challenge of their ideas is one of the causes of change in Europe and North America. At this time new universities and scientific societies are set up.

Voltaire

1700 powder-rooms appear in England for fashionable men and women to powder wigs and faces.

1703 First Russian newspaper, *Moskovskya Vyedomosti,* is published.

1704 First American newspaper, *Boston Newsletter,* is published.
1709 Russian prisoners sent to Siberia for the first time.
1714 German Gabriel Fahrenheit, makes a mercury thermometer.

THE AMERICAS

1732 Georgia, the last of the 13 colonies, is founded.

1721 Sir Robert Walpole becomes the first British Prime Minister and helps to transfer power to elected representatives. His home is 10 Downing Street, now the Prime Minister's official residence.

Maria Theresa Empress of Austria r.1740-1780 After fighting two wars against Prussia and France to keep the Habsburg Empire of Austria, Hungary and Bohemia under her control, Maria Theresa makes her capital city Vienna an important centre of painting, architecture and music, by her patronage.

1755 Destruction of Lisbon. A nine minute earthquake reduces Lisbon, fine and prosperous Portuguese capital, to rubble.

1739 Persian Conquests. Nadir Shah, the most successful of all Persian warriors, conquers western India and the Punjab and captures Delhi.

1757 Battle of Plassey. The army of Sirajuddaula, Nawab, or ruler, of Bengal in north-eastern India, is defeated by British troops led by Clive.

ASIA 1751-67 Manchu Power. Emperor Chi'ien Lung expands Chinese Empire to Tibet, Turkestan and Burma.

AFRICA

1728 Vitus Bering, a Danish explorer sent by Peter the great of Russia, finds a narrow gap between America and Asia, which is now called Bering Strait.

1735 Swedish botanist, Carolus Linnaeus, invents a new scientific method for naming plants and animals.

Rousseau

1730 Peak of the Rococo style of architecture and design, based on curves. Begun in France, it is very elegant and elaboure.
1730 John and Charles Wesley start Methodism.
1747-1755 Dr Samuel Johnson publishes his *Dictonary of the English Language.* In France, Diderot is compiling the *Encyclopédie.*
1736 French surgeon, Aymand, performs the first successful operation for appendicitis, called an appendectomy.
1738 First cuckoo clocks appear in mid-Europe.

1759 General Wolfe, leading the British army in capturing Quebec from the French, is killed in battle.

1755-1763 Seven Years' War. Britain joins Prussia in a war against France and Austria. Britain's quarrel with France is about the control of North American and Indian colonies. The Peace of Paris of 1763 gives Britain control of Canada and many Caribbean Islands.

Federick the Great, King of Prussia r.1740-1786 During Frederick's reign Prussia doubles in size and becomes the strongest Germanic power after Austria, due to a strong and well disciplined army. Influenced by the ideas of the Enlightenment, Frederick modernizes the country without losing any of his power.

1750-1782 James Watt, a Scotsman, invents the steam engine and develops ways to use it to power machinery.

1742 America. Russians explore Alaska.

c.1725 Italian composer Vivaldi, writes *The Four Seasons.* He composes over 400 concertos in his lifetime.

1726 Jonathan Swift, an Irishman, writes *Gulliver's Travels.*

1752 American statesman, scientist, inventor and author, Benjamin Franklin, announces his most important invention the lightning conductor, which proves the existence of electricity.

1764 Austrian composer, Mozart, a great musical genius, writes his first symphony at the age of eight.

Mozart

Johann Sebastian Bach 1685-1750 German composer, one of the greatest of all time, composes his most famous work, the religious oratorio, *St Matthew Passion,* in 1729. Many of his children are also composers and musicians.

1763 Pit-ponies are first used in mines.

1763 Chief Pontiac, from Ottowa, leads four Indian tribes in rebellion against the British. Even though he loses, his rebellion forces the British to negotiate a peace treaty.

1770 Boston Massacre. Americans become increasingly unhappy as British demand high taxes and deny them any say in Government. British soldiers shoot at protestors in Boston, killing five of them.

1773 Boston Tea Party. One thousand Bostonians stage a protest against the British tax on imported tea. Dressed as Indians, they board British ships loaded with tea and fling hundreds of tea chests into the sea.

1762-1796 Catherine the Great, born a German princess, overthrows her husband and reigns as Empress of Russia. She allows religious freedom, encourages learning and extends her empire.

1773-1775 Russian Serfs, whose lives become harder under Catherine the Great, revolt against their masters, led by the Cossack Pugachev, but the rebellion fails.

1772-1795 Poland Loses Independence as Prussia, Austria and Russia divide the country between themselves.

1770s Slave Trade at its height with several hundred thousand Black Africans a year taken across the Atlantic. As many as two-thirds die on board ship. Traders make big profits, but world opinion begins to move against slavery.

1766-1768 French explorer, Bougainville, discovers Polynesia and Melanesia.

1770s As tea becomes the favourite drink in Britain and Russia, 10,000 tons of Chinese tea are exported each year. Tea is very expensive and people keep it locked away.

1772 James Bruce, Scotish explorer, follows the course of the river Nile to Khartoum.

1774 Austrian Franz Mesmer uses hypnosis, which he called "mesmerism', for medical purposes.

Industrial Revolution 1750-1850. In Britain, men use new steam-powered machines for weaving and spinning cloth and, around the same time, iron production is improved. People flock from farms and villages to work the new buildings called "manufactories" and the first industrial towns grow up. Steam power starts to be used for engineering and transport, making Britain "the workshop of the world".

1775 German poet and dramatist, Goethe, begins writing his masterpiece *Faust.*

Canaletto 1697-1768 This Italian painter is known in particular for pictures of his home city of Venice.

1770 First public restaurant, "The Silver Tower" opens in Paris. It is still open today.

1779 First medical clinic for children opens in London.

American War of Independence

1775-1783 Americans declare war on Britain in a bid for independence. Led by George Washington, they beat British troops at Lexington and Concord in 1775 but lose the Battle of Bunker Hill the same year.

1776 Declaration of Independence is drawn up by Thomas Jefferson and signed on 4 July, in Philadelphia, by American Congress representing the 13 colonies.

1778-1779 French, Dutch and Spanish Join War on the side of the colonies to fight the British, whose troops finally surrender at Yorktown in 1781.

1783 Treaty of Par[is] This results in Brit[ish] recognition of the independence of t[he] 13 colonies, which later become the "United States of America".

1783 Peruvian Rev[olt] Tupac Amaru, nam[ed] after the last Inca rebels against the Spanish, but is def[eated] and executed.

French Revolu[tion] 1789-17[...]

1784 India Act. British government takes over political control of India from the East India Comp[any].

1780-1786 Japanese Famine. A great famine kills at least one million people. The famine followed by rice riots in 1787.

1782 King Rama I of Siam, now Thailand, moves his capital to Bangkok. Under his rule Siam grows richer and stronger. During the next century it is the only country in South Ea[st] Asia not taken over by Europeans.

1770 Dutch Settlers in South Africa move north fro[m] their colony at the Cape of Good Hope and fight Bantu peoples for their land in the first Kaffir war.

James Cook 1728-1779. British navigator, James Cook, explores the Pacific Islands and claims the east coast of Australia for Britain. He finds many anima[ls] and plants not known in Europe. Captain Cook is the first person to cross the Antarctic Circle. Durin[g] one of his voyages he is killed in Hawaii.

1777 French scientist, Antoine Lavoiser, founder of modern chemistry, discovers that air consists of oxy[gen] and nitrogen, and in 1790 produces the first table of chemical elements. He is executed during the Frenc[h] Revolution.

Romantic Movemen[t] 1770s-1820s Some poets, painters, musicians and artists reject the idea of "reason" and say feelings are more important. Romantic[...]

J.W. Goethe

1783 First successful [flight] in a hot-air balloon is undertaken by the French Montgolfier brothers.

1791 Canada Act divides Canada into English and French speaking territories.

1791 Slave Revolt. Toussaint l'Ouverture, a black slave, leads a revolt in Haiti and becomes governor of the Island.

1805 British Admiral Nelson defeats a French fleet at Trafalgar, but is killed in the battle.

1834 Tolpuddle Martyrs. Six English workers are transported to Australia after trying to set up a trade union.

9 **First American ...sident.** Great war ..., George ...hington, becomes ...sident of the United ...es of America.

... angry people of Paris revolt against ... taxes and the extravagant king, ... XVI. They tear down the hated ...lle Prison and declare ...ce a republic, in 1792. ... tries to escape but ... he and his ...en, Marie ...oinette, ... tried and ...eaded.

3-1794 **Reign of Terror.** The Jacobins, a new ...p, seize power under their leader, Robespierre. ...y kill all who disagree with them, beheading ...00 people in one year. They abolish ...stianity and rename the months and days. In ...end, they lose control and are themselves ...eaded.

...poleon Conquers ...rope 1792-1815. ...poleon Bonaparte, a ...liant young French ...neral, rises to lead the ...nch army. He wins ...ny wars and conquers ...ch of Italy in ...6 and Egypt ...798.

8 **"First Fleet"** of ...pean settlers ...e in Australia led by ...tain Arther Phillip. ...ing Botany Bay ...uitable, they move ...ydney. Half are ...oners from Britain. ... German astrologer, ...rick Herschel, discovers ...lanet Uranus, using ...flective telescope. ... English doctor, ...rd Jenner, first ...nates for smallpox.

... nature and the ...rnatural. English ...s, Wordsworth, ...n, Keats and ...ly and Polish ...ician, Chopin ...art of this ...ement.

7 Dollars are first ...d as currency in the ... trade.

8 First convicts are ...sported to Australia.

2 Denmark is the first country to ban the ...e trade.

4 Telegraph line is installed, between Paris ... Lille, France.

7 Frenchman André Garnerin demonstrates a ...chute, following a leap from a hot-air balloon.

1803 Great Land Sale. USA increases in size when its government buys the Louisiana Territory from Napoleon Bonaparte and the French, for $15 million.

Emperor Napoleon 1804-1821 Napoleon crowns himself Emperor of France in 1804 and becomes very popular. He controls almost all Western Europe by 1812 and, in the same year, mounts an invasion of Russia. However, the bitter Russian winter drives him back and many of his soldiers die during the campaign. Napoleon is finally beaten by British and German armies at Waterloo, in 1815, and he dies in exile in 1821.

1821-1832 Greek War of Independence. With support from Russia, Austria and Britain, the people of Greece win freedom from the Ottoman Empire.

1812-1859 Australian Settlement. Britain uses Australia as a place to send criminals. Later, free people sail to Australia, attracted by farmland and gold. They farm sheep and cattle, and take over the hunting grounds of native Aborigines. The white population grows from a few thousand to one million.

1840 New Zealand. The Treaty of Waitingi, between Maori chiefs and the British Governor, makes New Zealand a British possession.

1818 Shaka the Great forms the Zulu Empire in Southern Africa and drives other tribes northwards. Zulus are fierce, well organized fighters.

1794 Qaja Dynasty, Persia, is founded by Aga Muhammad. The dynasty lasts until 1925.

1799 Tipu Sahib, Sultan of Mysore from 1782 to 1799 and last independent ruler in South India, proclaims his defiance of the British.

1795 Mungo Park, from Scotland, traces the course of the River Niger.

1804-1806 Meriwether Lewis and William Clark travel with Indian guides from the east to the west coast of Africa.

Railways 1800s At the start of the century, engineers like Trevithick and Stephenson develop the first successful steam trains. In 1825 the first passenger railway opens in England. People fear that the human body cannot survive high speeds but the trains soon become a popular means of transport. By 1900 there are rail lines across the USA, Russia, India, Europe and China.

1790s Printing of books and coloured woodblocks reaches a high point in Japan with the work of the artist, Katsushika Hokusai.

1793 The Louvre, formerly a royal palace, becomes the national museum and art gallery of France.

Ludwig van Beethoven 1770-1827 This great German composer becomes deaf at the end of his life and never hears some of his finest music.

C.1800 Alessandro Volta invents the first electric battery. In honour of his discovery, electric units are called volts.

Simon Bolivar 1783-1830. Inspired by the American and French revolutions, and by L'Ouverture's slave revolt, Simon Bolivar, "The Liberator" helps lead the South American people in wars of independence and forces the Spanish government to give up Colombia, Venezuela and Peru. Bolivia is named after him.

1840s Child Labour. Young children work long hours in mines and in the new cloth factories. The government passes a series of laws which seek to protect children.

1846-1851 Irish Famine. Disease ruins the potato crop, an important food of the Irish people, and many people die of starvation and illness. During the 1800s many more sail to America and other places to start a new life.

CHINA 1839-1842 Opium War. Chinese fight to stop the British selling opium to the Chinese people. When China loses, Britain forces them to hand over control of Hong Kong.

Chinese ships, called junks, under attack.

AUSTRALASIA

1844-1848 Maori Uprisings against the British fail.

1850 Australian Colonies are given freedom to have their own governments.

1851 Australia. Gold is dicovered in the state of Victoria and people rush there to make their fortunes.

AFRICA

1835-1838 Great Trek of the Boers. The Boers, Dutch settlers living in South Africa, set off to find new lands and set up colonies in Natal, Orange Free State and the Transvaal. In 1838 they defeat the Zulus at the Battle of Blood River, Natal.

Exploring Africa 1800s. Following the great rivers, Europeans begin to travel across Africa. A British doctor, David Livingstone, travels north from South Africa across the Kalahari desert and then 1,500 miles west to the Atlantic Ocean. The journalist Stanley goes in search of him.

1847-1931 Thomas Edison, an American scientist, patents over 1,000 inventions, among them the record player, the microphone and the electric light bulb.

Edison's mechanical phonograph

1800s More people than ever can now read. Great story writers like Tolstoy in Russia, Dickens in Britain and Balzac in France, become very popular.

1830s "From Today Painting is Dead." French inventor, Niepce, develops the new process called photography. In 1888, the Kodak company begins selling small box cameras to the general public.

1829 Louis Braille, a French inventor, musician and teacher of the blind, himself blind from the age of three, publishes his system of finger reading for the blind which is named after him.

Mystery and Adventure 1840-1880. American writer Edgar Allan Poe's mysterous tales become very popular on both sides of the Atlantic. In France, Jules Verne's early science fiction stories include *Journey to the Center of the Earth.*

1830s-1900 Growth of USA continues as millions of settlers arrive from Europe. Many pioneers move west looking for land to farm and take the hunting grounds of the Native Americans by force. After many years of terrible fighting, the natives lose their last big battle at Wounded Knee, in 1890, and are herded into reservations. Small towns grow into big cities and the first skyscraper is built in Chicago in 1885.

1846-1848 Mexico Loses War against the USA and surrenders California, New Mexico, Utah and Colorado to the USA in return for a payment of $15 million.

1848 Californian Gold Rush. Many people hurry to California hoping to find a fortune after gold is found in some stream beds.

Year of Revolution 1848 Throughout Europe people rise up against their governments. In France, Germany, Italy, Austria, Hungary and Poland citizens force their rulers to make many changes. The French King, Louis Philippe, and the Austrian Emperor, Ferdinand, are forced to abdicate. In the same year Marx and Engels publish the *Communist Manifesto,* a book which forms the basis of modern communism.

1850-1864 Chinese Rebellions break out all over the country. Up to 20 million are killed in the fighting.

1856 First Steamship Company sets up a regular service between England and Australia.

Medical Revolution 1840s-1890s Scientific discoveries lead to big improvements in health care. American doctors start using ether and chloroform to put patients to sleep before operations. Queen Victoria uses it for childbirth. French chemist Pasteur discovers that germs cause disease and can spread from person to person. The invention of X-rays in 1895 means that doctors can see inside the human body.

1842 British Captain Ross maps 1,000 miles of Antarctic coastline.

1853 Irish Explorer, Richard Burton, disguises himself as an Arab and enters the Muslims' holy city of Mecca, which is forbidden to outsiders.

1846 Smithsonian Institution, one of the earliest national museums, opens in Washington, DC.

1851 Great exhibition of culture and industry, patronized by Prince Albert, is held in London in the Crystal Palace, a huge glass house. Six million people come to see exhibits from many lands. Its success leads to other national exhibitions in towns and cities all over the world.

THE AMERICAS

Abraham Lincoln

American Civil War 1861-1865 In the south, thousands of black slaves work for land-owners. Eleven southern states set up their own country, the Confederate States of America. Americans of the northern states fight to keep the south as part of the states of America. Over 600,000 Americans are killed in the war. Victory for the north means the end of slavery. In 1865 President Abraham Lincoln is assassinated while at the theatre.

1867 USA Buys Alaska from the Russians for $7 million.

Timeline continues on page 34

EUROPE

Queen Victoria r.1837-1901 While she is Queen, Britain comes to control nearly one-quarter of the world's population. In 1877 Victoria becomes the Empress of India. Through her nine children and thirty-one grandchildren, she is related to nearly all the royal families in Europe.

1854-1856 Crimean War. Russians try to take control of part of the Ottoman Empire, called Crimea. Turkey, France and Britain fight them to prevent it. The war kills many men. A young English woman, Florence Nightingale, later called "The Lady with the Lamp", goes out to nurse the sick and saves many lives.

1861 Freedom for Russian Serfs. Alexander II announces that serfs will no longer be sold like slaves and can now earn wages.

1860-1870 United Italy. People of small Italian states win freedom from French and Austrian control and form one united country. An Italian patriot, Garibaldi, leads 1,000 men, called "Red Shirts", in a successful fight to conquer Naples and Sicily.

1881 Russia. Revolutionaries kill Alexander II of Russia.

Rise of German Empire 1866-1900 Prussian Prime Minister Otto von Bismack, leads German state of Prussia in three successful wars against Denmark, Austria and France. Other German states join Prussia to form a united Germany, with King Wilhelm I as their first *Kaiser* or emperor. By 1900, Germany has a very large army.

1883 Russian Marxist Party is set up.

Garibaldi,

ASIA

INDIA

1857-1858 Indian Fight for Independence. After the outbreak of the Indian Mutiny fighting spreads through northern India. The British win back control at Lucknow and start to control India directly, through a governor. The Mogul dynasty comes to an end.

1862-1908 Empress Tzu Hui rules China. She dislikes European influence in China and resists attempts to modernize her country.

1868 Modernization of Japan. Shogunate dynasty ends when young Prince Mejii, fifteen, becomes emperor, and Japan begins to modernize.

1860s-1890s Indo-China. French take control of many countries in South-East Asia, including Cambodia and Laos. They call their colonies Indo-China.

1880 Ned Kelly, Australia's most famous bandit, is captured and hanged.

1882 Refrigerated Cargo ships make it possible for meat from New Zealand to be carried all over the world.

AUSTRALASIA

1868 Transportation of the prisoners from Britain to Australia ends.

The Scramble for Africa 1880-1914 In 1880 most of Africa is still ruled by African peoples. Then the European nations decide they want more possessions overseas. By 1914 the British, Germans, French, Belgians and Portuguese have come to control almost the whole continent.

1859-1868 Suez Canal is built by a French company in Egypt. Now sea travellers can sail between Europe and Asia without going around Africa.

1880-1902 Anglo-Boer Wars. Boers and British fight over how South Africa should be governed.

AFRICA

1860-1861 Robert Burke and William Wills cross Australia from south to north on camels but die on their way back.

1885 Benz of Germany builds the gasoline-driven car. People are fascinated but only the rich can afford them.

1866 Swedish chemist, Alfred Nobel, invents dynamite. He leaves his fortune to be given as prizes for scientific discoveries, peace and literature. These Nobel Prizes are still awarded each year.

1859 English naturalist Charles Darwin publishes the *Origin of Species*, which introduces the theory of natural selection. Later, in *The Descent of Man*, (1871) he suggests that humans shared an ancestor with the apes. Many people, especially churchmen, are outraged.

1860 French engineer, Etienne Lenoir, invents the first practical internal-combustion engine.

1874 First Impressionist exhibition is held in Paris. French artists try to capture natural light in their paintings. Many art critics dislike the new style.

1890 Dutch painter Vincent Van Gogh dies penniless. His now famous pictures use colour and brush marks to express feeling.

1889 Eiffel Tower is completed for the Paris Exhibition. At 984 ft (295m) it remains the world's tallest building for 40 years.

Golden Age of Children's Books 1860s Fairy tales by Danish writer Hans Christian Andersen help to create a demand for children's books. In 1861 Louisa May Alcott, an American, writes a book based on her own family, *Little Women*. It makes a great change from the usual "improving" books and is tremendously successful. In 1865 Lewis Carroll, a mathematician, writes *Alice's Adventures in Wonderland*, a work of great imagination.

1851 Singer, an American, builds the first sewing machine for use in the home.

1863 International Red Cross is set up in Switzerland to provide medical help for all people injured in wars.

1863 First military submarine is built for use in the American Civil War.

1873 Remington Co. in USA mass-produces first modern typewriter.

1874 In San Francisco, J. Davis and Levi Strauss make the first blue jeans with rivets.

1876 Alexander Graham Bell, a Scotsman, makes the first telephone.

1886 American, Dr J. Pemberton, first sells his new drink, Coca-Cola, as a "brain tonic".

1896 First modern Olympic games is held in Athens.

AD1700 TO AD1900 ~ EMPIRES AND DISCOVERY

CAPTAIN JAMES COOK

The famous British navigator and explorer, James Cook, was also an excellent mathematician, geographer and scientist. He explored the Pacific, visiting many islands, and charting the coasts of New Zealand and eastern Australia. The observations made during his voyages added greatly to the knowledge of the time and he was elected a Fellow of the Royal Society.

When he sailed around the world in the *Endeavour*, Cook was accompanied by many scientists, including the naturalist Joseph Banks, who studied and collected many of the plants they discovered. Botany Bay in Australia, where Cook landed in 1770, was given its name because of the large number of plant species found there.

On a later expedition, which set out in 1772, he became the first person known to have sailed southwards below the Antarctic Circle. His last voyage, in the *Discovery*, took him to the Hawaiian group of islands in 1778 and it was on Hawaii that he met his death in 1779, in a skirmish with the islanders.

THE GOLD RUSH

In the winter of 1847-48 John Augustus Sutter, busy with the building of a sawmill near the Sacramento River in California, discovered gold. Before long, thousands of farmers, miners, soldiers and trappers were scurrying west, along with many others unused to living in primitive conditions, such as school teachers and lawyers.

About 80,000 hopeful people arrived in 1849 and 77,760,000 grams (about 2,700,000 ounces) of gold was bought in just one year. New towns and cities sprang up 'overnight'.

Ten years later there was a second gold rush when Cherokee Indians struck gold in the Arkansas River area in Colorado. However, it is perhaps the gold rush in 1898, in the Klondike, that is most remembered because the conditions were so severe. Despite icy cold weather, prospectors extracted millions of dollars worth of gold - $22,000,000 in just one year in 1900.

There were similar scenes in Australia too, where actual nuggets of gold, rather than dust or grains, were to be found. The largest nugget found in Australia at that time weighed 165 lb (75 kg), while in South Africa, both gold and diamond mines created the same kind of rivalry and excitement.

It was the lure of gold that tempted many settlers to travel west and seize Indian lands. When gold was found in the Black Hills of Dakota, the Sioux and their leader, Sitting Bull, resisted the white man's advance.

CATHERINE THE GREAT

Catherine II, empress of Russia, was crowned in Moscow in September 1762 and reigned for 34 years. A German princess, married to Tsar Peter III of Russia, she deposed her mad husband who was murdered soon afterwards. She was a clever, strong and ambitious ruler and her reign added greatly to the power of Russia. She waged war against Sweden and Turkey, made deals with Prussia, captured the Crimea and the Black Sea coast and was in control of most of Poland. Catherine made many reforms, encouraged education for girls as well as for boys and established a system of medical care for the sick and needy. She wrote plays, collected works of art and cleverly manipulated her many passionate male admirers. To achieve all this she rose at 5am and often worked for 15 hours a day.

TOP: *Napoleon on the battlefield of Eylan, east Prussia, 1807. Painting by Baron A.G. Gross.* ABOVE: *Queen Victoria and Prince Albert at the opening ceremony of the Crystal Palace Exhibition at Hyde Park, London 1851. Painting by Henry Selous*

NATIVE AMERICANS

Prior to 1600, a million native Americans speaking 2000 languages, lived north of the Rio Grande. Construction of the railroad in 1838 cut across the buffalo herd trail and so destroyed the basis of their way of life.

At first the rights of native Americans were respected, but the Indian Removal Act of 1830 forced many from their land and some 100,000 went westward. Expelled from the south, 50,000 Cherokee were put into concentration camps; many died when they were marched to Oklahoma reservations in the winter of 1838.

> **Did you know that...**
>
> Native Americans were called 'Red Indians' because, when Columbus first landed in America, he believed he had reached India.
>
> The tomahawk was a ceremonial object used in tribal councils when matters of war and peace were settled; this is why when people settle an argument we say they are burying the hatchet.

CHILDREN AT WORK

Chimney sweeps

In the 18th century it was considered quite normal for young children to be trained to climb up inside chimneys to clean them. Even after the first Act of Parliament was passed to try and reduce this cruelty, a report in 1817 claimed there were about a thousand boy chimney sweeps, half of them working in London. They were apprenticed at four to eight years of age: some were sold by their parents; others were paupers that the parish no longer wanted to support. The boys suffered from falls, sores on their elbows and knees, and risked suffocation, especially in large buildings where a lot of soot had gathered. Sometimes girls were sent up the chimneys too, especially if their fathers happened to be sweeps.

Factories

Children worked long, gruelling hours for miserably low wages in very difficult conditions. Many seldom saw daylight. Some factories kept the machinery going day and night so one shift of children slept in the beds of those who were working. With the machinery unguarded and the children very tired after working fourteen hours or so, accidents and injuries were common. They were treated very strictly, in many cases brutally, but were constantly in fear of losing their jobs since there were many other poverty-stricken people desperate for work and ready to fill their places.

The coal mines

In the mid 1800s boys and girls worked undergroumd in coal mines. The hours were long, at least twelve and sometimes as many as eighteen hours a day for six days a week. Some of the children worked as trappers, filling the skips and carriages; others as pushers of the trucks; many were actually harnessed to these and had to drag the heavy loads behind them, crawling on all fours along the passages. The worst conditions were inflicted on apprentices from the workhouses.

Trolley-boys in an English mine.

QUEEN VICTORIA'S CHILDREN

Victoria's line spreads into many of Europe's royal families

Queen Victoria (1819-1901) (reign 1837-1901) married Albert of Saxe-Coburg-Gotha (1819-61)	Wilhelm II, born 1859, German Emperor married Augusta of Schleswig-Holstein-Augustenburg
	Seven other children
Victoria, the Princess Royal, born 1840 married Frederick III Crown Prince of Prussia (later German Emperor)	Albert Victor, Duke of Clarence, born 1864
	George, Duke of York, born 1865, **King George V of England**
The Prince of Wales, born 1841, **King Edward VII** of England married Alexandra of Denmark	Louise, born 1867
	Victoria, born 1868
Princess Alice, born 1843, married Louis IV. Grand Duke of Hesse-Darmstadt	Maud, born 1869, married **King Haakon of Norway**
	Alix, born 1872, married **Nicholas II Tzar of Russia**
Prince Alfred, born 1844, Duke of Edinburgh and Saxe-Coburg-Gotha married Marie of Russia	Five other children
	Four other children
Princess Helena, born 1846, became Princess Christian of Schleswig-Holstein	Marie, born 1875, married **Ferdinand of Romania**
Princess Louise, Duchess of Argyll, born 1848	Margaret, born 1882, married **King Gustav of Sweden**
	Two other children
Prince Arthur, Duke of Connaught, born 1850, married Louisa of Prussia	Victoria Eugenie, born 1887, married **King Alfonso of Spain**
Prince Leopold, Duke of Albany, born 1853, Princess Beatrice born 1857 married Henry of Battenberg	Three other children

NAPOLEON BONAPARTE (1769-1821)

Born on the island of Corsica in 1769, Napoleon was a soldier who rose to become Emperor of France in 1804. He was very successful and ambitious campaigner, and conquered Italy, Spain, Egypt, the Netherlands, and most of central Europe, despite being defeated by Nelson at the Battle of the Nile in 1798 and at Trafalgar in 1805. His armies swept across Europe, completely changing the political map. However, his Russian campaign in 1812, was a complete disaster. The Russians retreated, scorching the earth to leave no supplies behind them but drawing Napoleon ever further on. After a savage battle at Borodino, the French forces entered Moscow but found it abandoned and on fire. As they withdrew, matters were made worse by the onset of an early and harsh winter. Of the 453,000 soldiers who had set out, only 10,000 returned fit to fight again. After these defeats, Napoleon was exiled on Elba but he escaped to rule France again for a hundred days.

He mustered an army to fight the Prussians, and the British at Waterloo in 1815 - a hard-fought battle which he very nearly won. Defeated and overthrown, he was made a prisoner on the island of St Helena.

As well as being such a brilliant general, he introduced new laws and reforms in France that were copied in many other countries. He reorganized France in the wake of the French Revolution and although his Empire was destroyed many of his ideas lived on.

THE NEW WORLD

Western Europe was quick to colonize and conquer the newly discovered American continents. The Spanish rapidly overthrew the Aztec and Inca empires, creating a vast empire of their own and growing rich on huge sources of gold and siilver. Catholic Christianity spread with them, while Protestant Christians - Dutch, French and British - colonized North America. During the 18th century, Britian won the struggle with France for control of the new lands. However, the principal colonies soon declared themselves independent, becoming the United States of America by 1783 and leaving the north to become British Canada. During the early part of the 19th century, Spanish and Portuguese colonies began to establish independent states. Until recently, these states were often unstable, which tended to predispose them to authoritarian rule. By a combination of war and treaty, the USA extended the western frontier of occupation to the Pacific shore during the course of the 19th century. At the end of that century, following a traumatic Civil War, the USA became a full imperial power. Cuba and the Philippines were taken from Spain, and the USA entered the First World War in 1917. The nation had been filled out with immigrants from Europe and by the mid-20th century had become one of two 'superpowers'. The USA was vastly productive, with technical superiority that enabled her to put men on the Moon in 1969 and to lead the West against the Communist bloc during the Cold War (1945-1989).

EUROPE

The Ottoman Turks advanced to the gates of Vienna in 1683, briefly threatening Europe with another Islamic invasion. However, a greater threat to Christianity lay within Europe itself. During the 1520s, the Reformation split the Church and began to tear Europe apart. Religious wars between Catholic and Protestant states caused widespread death and destruction well into the 17th century. The 16th and 17th centuries saw modern centralized nation states emerging, their armies and fleets made more powerful by the use of gunpowder. Strong 'absolute' monarchs modelled themselves on the French king, Louis XIV (r.1643-1715), while the trading nations, Britain and the Netherlands, competed with France and Spain overseas. The state of Brandenburg-Prussia in Germany reached a high point under Frederick the Great.

• The newly-united Russian state expanded rapidly. The Russians annexed Kazan in 1552, Astrakhan in 1556, taking them to the mouth of the Volga, and in the 1570s, they reached the Urals. During the next decade, with the help of the Cossacks, they defeated the Khanate of Sibir, and by the mid-17th century were at the shore of the Pacific. Peter the Great (1682-1725) took the Baltic countries from Sweden and began to modernize and westernize the country. Catherine the Great (1762-1796) fought successful wars to extend Russia to the south, taking lands from the Turks. Poland, which had been Russia's oppressor in the first half of the 17th century, disappeared off the map during the late 18th century as it was partitioned by Russia, Prussia and Austria. Independence would come only briefly under Napoleon, and then again in the 20th century.

• European expansion reached around the world. Spain, Portugal, France and Britain established colonies in the New World. Portuguese traders entered the Indian Ocean and the Pacific. Dutch seafarers created an empire in the East Indies, while Britain and France were imperial rivals in India. During the later years of the 19th century, the continent of Africa was hastily carved up between hungry European powers, which now included Germany. The empires they created endured until the middle of the 20th century, to be swept away after the Second World War.

BELOW: In an attempt to stop Turkish reinforcements from Egypt getting through to Greece, which would have weakened the Greek Revolution against the Ottoman Turkish rule, a combined British, French and Russian naval force destroyed the Turkish and Egyptian fleet at Navarino harbour in 1827. This was the turning point in the fortunes of the once vast Ottoman Empire. Within a century, only Istanbul would remain part of Turkey.

BELOW: Apollo II astronaut Edwin Aldrin on the Moon, standing by the device set up to detect the solar wind. Behind him is the lunar module.

• The French Revolution (1789) set off a chain of wars in Europe that lasted a quarter of a century, with Napoleon Bonaparte briefly ruling a French Empire. After his fall in 1815, half a century of peace set in. Then, in 1870, Prussian armies united northern Germany to form the German Empire. Before long, Europe became two armed camps: Britain, France and Russia, faced by Germany and her southern neighbour, Austria-Hungary, which had united into a powerful new military state, and reached its high point under Frederick the Great.

WORLD WARS

The disintegration of the Ottoman Empire in Europe helped to ignite the First World War (1914-18) which killed 8 million people. After an uneasy peace, fascist Germany grew strong, annexed Austria and allied with the fascist regime in Italy. This plunged Europe into a Second World War (1939-45) which was even worse. This involved almost all the major nations of the world; over 50 million died, inlcuding 7 million Jews, systematically murdered by the Nazis.
After the war, the new state of Israel provided a homeland for the Jews but brought conflict with Arab neighbours, which had recently become independent after the break-up of the Turkish Empire.

• At the beginning of the third millennium, civil wars and oppression continue around the world. After the First World War, the League of Nations, founded in 1920 to prevent further wars, failed in its purpose. The United Nations, established in 1945, has had more success and has been deeply involved, by means of peacekeeping forces, health and welfare sub-organizations, in many emergencies around the globe, including in the former Yugoslavia.

Russian expansion during 16th and 17th centuries into 'Siberia'

1570s

URAL MTS

by 1604

1632
Yakutsk

1649 Okhotsk

Irkutsk

18th and 19th centuries

Late 17th-early 18th centuries, Chinese expansion to make buffer states (Mongolia, Tibet, etc) on borders

Kabul
BABUR
1526
PERSIA
(IRAN)
Delhi

HIMALAYAS

MOGHUL EMPIRE

JAPAN:
1603 Tokugawa dynasty united all Japan; peace and isolation for 2½ centuries (to 1911)

Yellow R.
Peking

Kyoto

...rid Persia zenith under ...ah Abbas the Great (1587-1629)

Moghul Empire founded by Babur (from Afghanistan) Zenith under Akbar (1556-1605) Great Moghul Aurangzeb (1658-1707) enlarged the empire. Thereafter Mahratta States became main enemies

CHINA
Ming Dynasty overthrown 1644 by Manchurian invaders: Manchu/ Ch'ing/Qing Dynasty (to 1911)

Burma

Siam Vietnam

PHILIPPINES
(Spanish to 1898)

Singapore

...A

...MALIA

...NIA

...AWI

MADAGASCAR

DUTCH EAST INDIES
(INDONESIA 1949)

DESERT AUSTRALIA

Melbourne Sydney

NEW ZEALAND
Wellington

CHINA

Early in the 17th century, Manchurian tribes began to assault the Great Wall and, by 1644, they had overthrown the Ming dynasty. The new Manchu or Ch'ing (Qing) dynasty was to survive until the 20th century. It reached its peak under Emperor K'ang Hsi (1662-1722) whose campaigns established 'buffer' states around the core empire. Mongolia was taken in 1696 and Tibet was incorporated in 1724. Within these vast boundaries, China pursued her own course, increasingly isolated and overtaken by Western progress.

By the 19th century, the Chinese Empire was in decay and prey to aggressive Western powers. However, Japan took the greatest advantage, annexing China's subject state, Korea, in 1904. The last Manchu emperor abdicated in 1912, and the civil war that followed gave Japan the opportunity to create an empire in Manchuria and northern China. Although she was liberated from invaders at the close of the Second World War, China lapsed into civil war again from 1946 to 1949. The Communist victors, who continue in power today, are at last opening the country to Western influences.

JAPAN

The Tokugawa shoguns, who were established in 1603, brought two centuries of peace to Japan. Western influences were excluded until the 1850s, when the country was opened up to trade. Japan then rapidly modernized and set out upon almost a century of aggression, against Korea, China and Russia (from the late 19th century to 1904). Then, in 1941, she entered the Second World War by capturing US and European Far Eastern colonies. Japan was ultimately brought to defeat by atomic weapons in 1945, but spent the next half century achieving astonishing economic success.

RUSSIA

In 1917, the Russian imperial regime was overthrown and Russia became a Communist republic. The German invasion of Russia during the Second World War did enormous damage but, under dictator Stalin, the Union of Soviet Socialist Republics emerged in 1945 in control of half Europe and as one of the world's two 'superpowers'. The confrontation between the USSR and Western democracies lasted more than 40 years and became known as the Cold War. Soviet military might faced the armed West across the 'Iron Curtain' in Europe, while pursuing power politics in the developing nations of the 'Third World'. In 1989, however, the Communist system failed in the USSR and it broke up. Eastern Europe celebrated its freedom, as did the new republics of central Asia.

INDIA

The Mogul emperor Babur (1494-1530) destroyed the Sultanate of Delhi in 1526 and took control of the states of northern India, and his empire was pushed southwards in the 17th century. Emperor Aurangzeb (1658-1707) extended this empire further, persecuting Hindus and provoking opposition from the Maratha states. India was again divided. In the 19th century, Britain established an Empire which lasted until 1947, when independence was granted to Muslim Pakistan and Hindu India. In 1971, Eastern Pakistan seceded, becoming Bangladesh.

...BOVE: The Harrier GR7 took part in the Nato ...rstrikes on Yugoslavia, during the Kosovo conflict ...1999. Utilising the full potential of a Forward ...cking Infra-Red sensor and Night Vision ...oggles, the British Harrier GR7 can operate ...pinpoint accuracy by day and night.

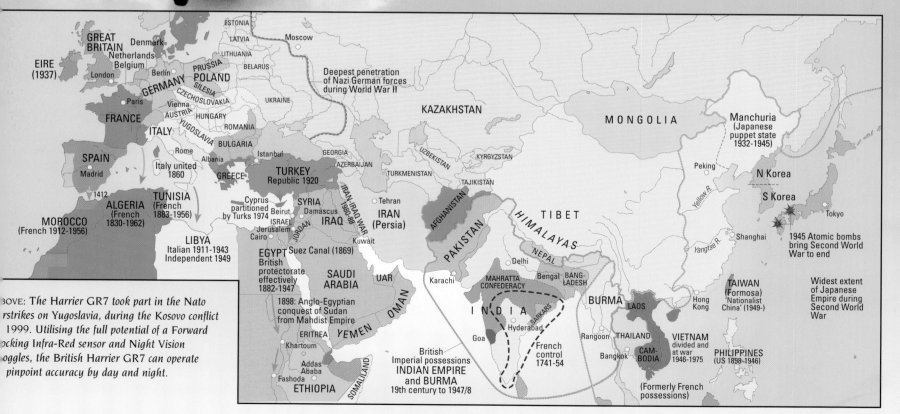

ESTONIA
LATVIA
GREAT BRITAIN Denmark
Moscow
EIRE (1937)
Netherlands LITHUANIA
London Belgium PRUSSIA BELARUS
Berlin POLAND
GERMANY SILESIA
Paris CZECHOSLOVAKIA UKRAINE
Vienna AUSTRIA HUNGARY
FRANCE YUGOSLAVIA ROMANIA

Deepest penetration of Nazi German forces during World War II

KAZAKHSTAN

MONGOLIA

Manchuria (Japanese puppet state 1932-1945)

ITALY
SPAIN BULGARIA
Rome
Madrid Italy united 1860 ALBANIA
GREECE
1412
TUNISIA (French 1883-1956)
ALGERIA (French 1830-1962)
MOROCCO (French 1912-1956)
LIBYA Italian 1911-1943 Independent 1949
Istanbul GEORGIA
TURKEY Republic 1920 AZERBAIJAN
Cyprus partitioned by Turks 1974
SYRIA Damascus Tehran
Beirut IRAN IRAQ WAR 1980-88
ISRAEL IRAQ IRAN (Persia)
Jerusalem JORDAN
Cairo Kuwait
EGYPT Suez Canal (1869)
British protectorate effectively 1882-1947
SAUDI ARABIA
UAR
1898: Anglo-Egyptian conquest of Sudan from Mahdist Empire
ERITREA YEMEN
OMAN
Khartoum
Addas Ababa
Fashoda
SOMALILAND
ETHIOPIA

UZBEKISTAN
TURKMENISTAN
KYRGYZSTAN
TAJIKISTAN
AFGHANISTAN
PAKISTAN HIMALAYAS TIBET
Delhi NEPAL
Karachi
MAHRATTA CONFEDERACY BANG-
Bengal LADESH
I N D I A
SARKARS
Goa Hyderabad
British Imperial possessions INDIAN EMPIRE and BURMA 19th century to 1947/8
French control 1741-54
(Formerly French possessions)

Peking
Yellow R.
N Korea
S Korea
Tokyo
Shanghai
1945 Atomic bombs bring Second World War to end
Yangtse R.
Hong Kong
TAIWAN (Formosa) 'Nationalist China' (1949-)
BURMA LAOS
Rangoon THAILAND VIETNAM divided and at war 1946-1975
Bangkok CAM- BODIA PHILIPPINES (US 1898-1946)
Widest extent of Japanese Empire during Second World War

THE AMERICAS

1906 San Francisco suffers a violent earthquake, costing $400m in property damage.

EUROPE

1911-1921 Mexico. After the overthrow of dictator, Diaz, revolutionary conflict lasts for ten years.

1914 Panama Canal opens, providing a 51 mile link that allows large ships passage between the Atlantic and Pacific Oceans.

1912 The Titanic, the largest passenger ship in the world, sinks on its first trip to New York, drowning 1,513 people.

1916 Dublin. British troops crush the Easter Rising of the Sinn Fein movement. The government executes many of the leaders, and thus creates support for the rebels.

1913 Suffragettes Protest. British women demonstrate to demand the same voting rights as men. During the First World War women work at the Front and in the armed forces, and take over other important jobs from men who have gone to fight.

1917 The USA joins the First World War. One million American soldiers fight with the Allied Powers. This is the first major involvement of US troops in Europe.

1920-1933 Prohibiton. Producing and selling alcohol is illegal. Gang bosses, like Al Capone, get rich from illegally selling alcohol. In big cities gangsters bribe the authorities to leave them alone.

1921 Irish Free State. Ireland is divided. Six of the nine Ulster counties in the North want to remain part of Great Britain. The South becomes a separate country, called the Irish Free State.

1929-1932 The Great Depression. After economic uncertainty in Europe, share prices suddenly fall on the New York stock market, an event known as the Wall Street "crash". Many banks and businesses close. By 1932, 12 million Americans are out of work. Unemployment and poverty affect the whole world, especially Germany and Japan.

1932 Franklin D. Roosevelt is elected President of the USA. "New Deal", when th State invests large su

1926 General Strike. Workers from many industries strike in protest at the hardshi caused by the econo depression.

The First World War 1914-1918

The power of the German Empire leads the European nations to form alliances. France, Great Britian and Imperial Russia become allies on one hand, and Germany and Austria-Hungary on the other. When the heir to the Austrian-Hungarian throne is assassinated in Serbia, his country threatens Serbia and is in turn threatened by Russia. Germany has to help Austria-Hungary, but knows that she will be attacked by Russia's ally, France. Germany therefore attacks France first.

Great Britain declares war on Germany, and Russia goes to war against Austria-Hungary and Germany. Most battles take place in Europe, although soldiers come from Canada, Africa, Australia, India and New Zealand to fight. For the first time armies use tanks and planes and trench warfare becomes important. In 1917 Russia leaves the war, but the USA joins the Allied Powers, helping them to win. According to the peace treaty, Germany must pay for the costs of the war.

1919 League of Nations. The horrors of the First World War cause many countries to form an association aimed at keeping world peace.

1919-1945 Italy. In 1919 Mussolini sets up the Fascist Party and becomes the dictator of Italy in 1922. Fascists believe that the government should have total control over people's lives, and that there should be no other political parties. Musssolini wants Italy to be the centre of a new Roman Empire.

1924 Stalin takes over control of the USSR when Lenin dies. He drives out Trotsky and remains dictator of Russia until 1953. He forces farming and industry to modernize and kills millions of people who oppose him. The secret police become very powerful.

1923 Turkey Becomes a Republic. First president is General Mustafa Kemal "Ataturk" who works hard to modernize his country. He introduces the Western alphabet to take the place of Arabic writing.

Adolf Hitler 1933-1945 Millions of Germans, made poor by the Depression and humiliated by the Versailles agreement of 1919, look for a strong leader. Hitler becomes the "Fuhrer leader, of Germany in 1933 and the Nazi p takes over the government. Nazis share m beliefs with the Fascists. Hitler hates Jews and gypsies and during the period known

Russian Revolution 1917

After many defeats in the First World War, the army and the people turn against Tsar Nicholas II. Eventually, the Bolsheviks, led by Lenin and Trotsky, seize power and set up a revolutionary government. They develop a Communist system based on the belief that factories and businesses should belong to the state and not to a few rich people. They call Russia the Union of Soviet Socialist Republics, USSR, and eventually ban all other political parties.

1905 Bloody Sunday. Imperial troops shoot Russian workers in St Petersburg.

ASIA AND AUSTRALASIA

Northern Teretory
Western Australia
Queensland
New South Wales
South Australia
Victoria
Tasmania

MIDDLE EAST

1901 Commonwealth of Australia brings together seven separate states into one country.

1910-1945 Korea. Japanese take control of Korea.

CHINA

1911 Sun Yat-Sen leader of the National People's Party sets up a republican government.

1918-1932 Arab States. Arabs set up new states, most ruled by princes or kings.

1919 Amritsar. Unarmed Indians hold demonstrations. British troops kill nearly 400 people.

1920 Mohandas Gandhi reorganizes the Indian National Congress Party. He believes violence is wrong and works to free India from British rule by peaceful protest and what he calls "civil disobedience". His followers name him "Mahatma" or the "Great Soul".

INDIA

1921 Mao Tse-Tung helps form Chinese Communist Party.
1934-35 Long March. When Nationalist rulers attack them, Mao Tse-Tung leads the Communists on a 6,000 mile march across China to safety. Fewer than one in ten survive the journey.

1931-1939 Japanese Expansion. After takin control of Manchuria i Northern China in 193 the Japanese begin al out war on China in 1937, bombing big cities and capturing Shanghai and Beijing.

1900 Austrian Sigmund Freud publishes *The Interpretation of Dreams.* His work helps doctors to understand the human mind.

1901 An Austrian scientist, Landsteiner, discovers human blood groups, allowing patients to be given matching blood.

1903 Marie and Pierre Curie receive the Nobel prize following their discovery of radium.

1900s Black musicians in the USA develop a new kind of music, jazz, based on the black experience of slavery and African music. It allows performers to experiment while they play. Among the best-known is Louis Armstrong.

1901 Flight of Count Zeppelin's airship.

1901 A British inventor, Booth designs the first electric vacuum cleaner.

1901 The Italian, Guglielmo Marconi, sends first radio signal across Atlantic Ocean.

1906 Kellogg sells Corn Flakes, the most popular cereal in the world.

1906 Norwegian explorer, Roald Amundsen, sails through the North-West passage from the Atlantic to Alaska.

1900s Cinema. From the beginning of the century cinema on both sides of the Atlantic becomes more popular. Hollywood creates silent movie stars like Charlie Chaplin and Greta Garbo. The first "talking picture" is "*The Jazz Singer*", 1927.

1907 The first Cubist Exhibition in Paris shows works influenced by Picasso. As artists become more and more experimental and "abstract", paintings and sculpture become difficult for people to understand.

1908 American, Henry Ford, makes the Model "T" car. By the end of 1913 his factory is turning out more than 1,000 cars a day.

1908 Lord Baden-Powell founds Boy Scouts.

1909 Leo Baekeland produces the first hard plastic made entirely from chemicals, Bakerlite.

1909 American Explorer Robert Peary is the first man to reach the North Pole.

1911 South Pole. Roald Amundsen wins the race to be the first man to reach the South Pole. Captain Scott and his British team arrive one month later, but die on the way back from cold and hunger.

1913 Hans Geiger, a German physicist, invents a counter for measuring radioactivity.

1913 Revolutionary performances by dancers, including that by Nijinsky in *The Rite of Spring*, shock some audiences who dislike the modern music and movements.

1911 The first air mail flight is made to India.

1914 Traffic lights, which are only red and green, are put up in the USA.

Conquest of the Air 1903-1939

American brothers, Orville and Wilbur Wright, build the first successful airplane in 1903. Their biplane Flyer I flies for 850 feet. Britons, Alcock and Brown, make the first non-stop flight across the Atlantic in 1919 Meanwhile European inventors design the first helicopters.

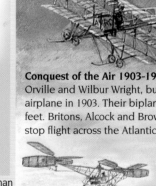

1920 Radio broadcasting begins in the USA. People can listen to their favourite performers in their own homes.

1919 The Bauhaus Movement begins in Germany, aiming to use new technological discoveries to improve design and architecture.

1922 Tomb of ancient Egyptian King Tutankhamen is re-discovered by archaeologists Howard Carter and Lord Carnarvon.

1923 Swedish scientists, von Platen and Munters, design the first electric refrigerator.

Nuclear Physics 1900-1954

New ideas about how energy and light behave and what atoms are made lead scientists to look at nature differently. The wo of men like Ernest Rutherford, Max Planck and Albe Einstein in the early 1900s lead to the developme of the atomic bomb in 1945 and the first nuclear power station in 1954.

1934 William Beebe and Otis Barton desce to 3,048 feet under Atlantic Ocean in a steel ball called a bathysphere.

1930s When the Nazis burn books and close theatres in Germany, m writers, artists and musicians move to the

1926 A Norwegian, Rotheim, invents the aerosol, which allows all kinds of liquid to be sprayed in a fine mist.

1928 The first antibiotic drug, Penicillin, is discovered by Scottish scientist, Alexander Fleming. Antibiotics can destroy bacteria that cause many diseases.

1928 Walt Disney makes first Mickey Mouse cartoon.

1928 The first electric razor appears in the USA.

1930s Comic books become popular in the USA and two of the m famous heroes, Super and Batman, are creat

of money in public works, helps to create more jobs and offers better welfare pogramme for the unemployed.

6 Edward VIII gives is claim as king in er to marry the an he loves, Mrs son. This causes a political crisis.

holocaust he orders millions to be d in death camps. His dreams of ing Germany the strongest country in world lead to the Second World War.

-1939 Spanish Civil General Franco leads Spanish against the blican government. Fascist he receives from Hitler and solini. People from all the world form the national Brigade to fight against Franco, is army wins control he becomes dictator ain, 1939-1975.

Abyssinia. The Italian army invades the try, now Ethiopia, taking power from eror Haile Selassie, keeping it until 1941.

7 German airship Hindenburg is royed by fire in Jersey, USA.

Surrealist art, like Salvador Dali, is ed by dreams and les paintings, tures and films.

The British scientist, s, tests the first radar ce system. Using waves it can detect nes from miles away. The first nylon yarn de in the USA. It ces silk in the making ckings. The British cating Corporation s the first black-and-television service to ailable to all. Biro makes the first sfull ball-point pen.

1941 Pearl Harbour. After part of the Japanese air force bombs an American naval base, Pearl Harbour, the USA joins the Second World War.
1943 Argentina. A revolution makes Juan Perón ruler of his country. His wife, Evita, is very popular, especially among the poor.
1945 United Nations. In San Francisco 48 countries sign a charter and form the United Nations, whose aim is to settle arguments between countries peacefully.

1940-1945 Winston Churchill is Prime Minister. A great wartime leader he tells the British people "We shall fight on the beaches... we shall never surrender."

1944-1949 Greece. Civil war breaks out between the Communists and the supporters of the King. With help from Britain and the USA the Communists are defeated.

Second World War 1939-1945
Hitler sends the German army into Poland. England and France declare war but they cannot stop the Axis powers, Germany and Italy, from taking over most of Europe. Japan joins the Axis in 1940. Russia and America come into the war in 1941, both fighting against the Axis. War ends in Europe in May 1945, when the Germans surrender. Between 1939 and 1945, 55 million people are killed, 21 million in the USSR alone. More than half of the dead are not soldiers, but civilians including women and children.

1948-1949 Berlin. The Soviets cut off overland routes to Berlin. English and American planes fly in supplies. In 1949 Germany divides: it becomes the Federal Republic in the West and the Democratic Republic in the East. A wall is built through the middle of Berlin to stop people crossing from one side to the other.
1949 NATO. Many countries in Northern Europe join with Canada and the USA to form the North Atlantic Treaty Organization. Members share responsibility for defending each other's countries.

1948 Israel. The Jewish National Council proclaims the new state of Israel in the land once known as Palestine. Jewish people from all over the world go to live there. The Arab countries of Syria, Egypt and Jordan are against this. There are wars between Israel and its neighbours in 1949, 1967 and 1973. Palestinian Arabs, some still living in refugee camps forty years later, are bitter at losing their homeland.

1940-1945 Second World War. After joining the Axis, Japan takes over many countries in South East Asia and the Pacific. Three months after the war ends in Europe in 1945 America drops nuclear bombs on Hiroshima and Nagasaki. Only two of these terrible new weapons kill 80,000. Japan surrenders.

1947 India becomes independent of British rule. It divides into two countries, the Hindu state of India and the Muslim state of Pakistan. In fierce fighting between the two religious groups thousands are killed and millions must move their homes.

1950-1953 The Korean War, between North and South Korea, breaks out. The North is helped by the USSR, the South by the United Nations troops, which are mostly American. After the war ends the country remains divided.

1946-1949 Civil War Ends in a victory for the Communists. Mao Tse-Tung becomes leader of the People's Republic of China.

1947 Norwegian, Thor Heyerdahl, sails 4,000 miles across the Pacific Ocean on a raft made from balsa wood. His aim is to prove that South Americans could have settled the Pacific Islands.
1953 Edmund Hillary from New Zealand and Sherpa Tenzing from Nepal are the first people to reach the top of Mount Everest, the world's tallest mountain.
1940 Prehistoric wall paintings are discovered in caves in Lascaux, France.
1946 The first Cannes Film Festival takes place.

c.1942 An aqualung for deep-sea diving is designed by Frenchman Jacques Cousteau.

1948 South Africa. The Nationalist Party brings in a policy of apartheid (seperateness), where non-white people will have no real share in government, which is controlled by white people.

1948 The World Health Organization is set up. Its programme of vaccination helps to wipe out deadly diseases all over the world.

1947 *The Diary of Anne Frank* is published. (See key feature on page 37)
1948 George Orwell writes the novel 1984 which introduces the slogan "Big Brother is Watching you".

1952 Elizabeth II becomes Queen. Her coronation is the first national event to be seen by millions on television.

1957 Treaty of Rome. Six countries in Western Europe join to form the European Economic Community, EEC, or Common Market. The EEC helps its members to trade with each other and its aim is eventual European Union. Six more countries join between 1973 and 1983.

1958 Cuba. After six years of civil war, Fidel Castro becomes the first communist leader of Cuba.
1958-1969 France. General Charles de Gaulle, a hero of the Second World War, is President of the Fifth Republic.

1956 Hungary. The Russian army crushes an uprising against communism.

1958-1959 The Great Leap Forward. The government introduces many changes in farming and industry. The aim is to modernize factories and to produce enough food for millions of Chinese people.

1953 Crick and Watson work out the structure of DNA, a chemical compound found that is found inside all cells of all living things. Their discovery explains how new cells grow.

DNA

1950s Teenagers become identified with their own music, clothes and heroes. Film stars who gain worldwide popularity include the young and beautiful Brigitte Bardot, James Dean, and Marilyn Monroe.

1950 USA. Diners Club creates the first credit card.
1950 American surgeon, Richard Lawler, performs the first successful kidney transplant.
c.1953 An American company designs the first microwave oven.

1954 British athlete, Roger Bannister, is the first man to run a mile in under four minutes.

Clock in 1955, a new age in popular music begins for young people. The American singer, Elvis Presley, is their hero. He makes 170 hit records. In 1963, the Beatles, from Britain, have their first number one song and start a craze, "Beatlemania". Now top artists sell millions of discs, cassettes and videos all over the world.

Rock'n'Roll 1955-1990s With Bill Haley's *Rock Around the*

1962 Cuban Missile Crisis. The USSR sets up bases for nuclear weapons in Cuba. President Kennedy threatens to declare war if they are not removed. Soviet leader Khrushchev finally agrees.
1963 US President John F. Kennedy is assassinated in Dallas, Texas.

1968-1990 Northern Ireland. After the failure of a civil rights movement, violence breaks out again between Nationalists who want a united Ireland and Unionists, who wish to remain part of Britain. Republican terrorists renew conflict with security forces who have been sent to keep the peace.
1968 Czechoslovakia. When Czech leader, Dubcek, tries to introduce "Communism with a human face", Russian forces invade and remove him from power.

1964-1975 The Vietnam War. After the Vietnamese win independence from the French in 1954, fighting begins between Communist North and non-Communist South Vietnam. The USA and other countries send troops to help the South, but the Vietcong (Vietnamese Communists) are experts at jungle warfare. In 1973, US forces leave after eight years of fighting. Vietnam becomes one Communist country in 1975.

1966-1968 Cultural Revolution. Mao forms students into groups of Red Guards, who attack anything which they think might be against Communist ideas. Many people are killed or put in prison.

1954-1962 Algeria. Independence from French rule is won.
1956 Egypt. President Nasser says that the Suez Canal belongs to Egypt. British and French forces occupy the canal zone, but the United Nations demands that they leave.

1953 Colour television broadcasts begin in the USA.
1960s The birth control pill becomes widely available.

1960s A new opera house is built in Sydney, Australia. Special engineering techniques are needed for the unusual design.

1967 Vietnam Protests. As more American soldiers are killed in Vietnam, many people begin to demonstrate against the war.
1955-1968 Civil Rights Movement. Blacks in the southern states of America demand the right to be treated the same as white citizens. The Baptist minister, Martin Luther King, leads their peaceful protests until he is assassinated in 1968.

1960 The American, Theodore Maiman, builds the first machine to make a lazer beams.

1960 Sirimavo Bandaranaike of Ceylon, now Sri Lanka, becomes the world's first woman Prime Minister.

1962 The first industrial robots go on sale. They do factory work in place of humans.

1960s American Pop Artists including Andy Warhol, use popular images like soup advertisements in their art.

1962 Live satellite television broadcasts between the USA and Europe follow the launch of the Telstar communications satelitte.
1963 Valentina Tereshkova becomes first woman in space.

Cuba

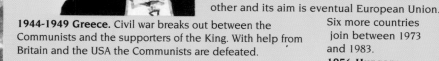

ABOVE: *A Royal Irish Fusilier teases a Turkish sniper at Gallipoli while his comrades are deep in the sleep of utter exhaustion.*

RIGHT: *Propaganda was a powerful tool during wartime and both sides used it to great effect. This selection shows how poster campaigns were waged to influence the way people thought about war.*

FACTS ABOUT THE FIRST WORLD WAR

• After Britain and France declared war on Turkey, T.E. Lawrence (known as Lawrence of Arabia) became involved in helping the British army in Egypt. Lawrence succeeded in capturing Aqaba and with Feisal, the Arab prince, helped take Damascus, leading his Arabian tribesmen in triumph through the streets, after much bitter fighting and an exhausting camel march across the Arabian desert.

• At Passchendaele, near Ypres (1917), torrential rain turned the battlefields into deep mud. After four months of trench warfare, the British troops gained only 5 miles (8 kilometres) of ground but lost 325,000 men.

• With wireless still in its infancy and field telephones often wrecked by shellfire or run over by wagons, the first military aircraft were used to check out enemy lines. In some places more primitive communications were used and carrier pigeons transported the messages. In 1916 one unfortunate bird, suffering from gas poisoning and exhaustion, dropped dead as it delivered its message in Verdun and became the only pigeon ever to be awarded the Legion of Honor.

• In 1917, 19 mines were detonated within 19 seconds of each other under German positions in Ploegsteert Wood, south of Ypres, creating huge craters and terrifying the German troops. Shock waves were felt as far away as London.

• German airships were used to drop bombs on British towns and on the night of 2nd-3rd September 1916, 14 airships dropped nearly 35,000 lb (15,750 kg) of bombs on many parts of England, including London.

BELOW: *On 15th September 1916, a carefully guarded secret was brought into the open, when for the first time British tanks went into action in the Battle of the Somme. The Germans were taken completely by surprise as a single tank with two companies of infantry cleared a mile of trench and took 370 prisoners with the loss of only five Allied men.*

• On 15 December, 1914, in one corner of the Western Front, the opposing armies were dug into trenches just a few yards apart, singing carols in recognition of Christmas Day. Speaking in simple French, the German soldiers suggested a temporary truce and met the English troops in the open to exchange their cigars for English jam.

• Tanks were used for the first time in the Battle of the Somme in 1916. Once off the roads they could move at just over half a mile (one kilometre) an hour and many of them broke down or were ditched. Only nine of the forty-nine that set out actually reached the German trenches at the right time but these certainly created a panic among the enemy who had no warning that these strange armoured monsters would appear!

FACTS ABOUT THE SECOND WORLD WAR

• In May 1940 at Dunkirk, on the northern coast of France, some 338,226 Allied troops, apparently trapped after being driven back to the coast by the German army, were rescued and returned to England in all manner of craft, from destroyers and cross-channel steamers to small fishing boats and river cruisers.

• Sometimes airborne operations were carried out, not just by parachutists, but by men in gliders. In 1944 at Arnhem in Holland, 13,781 men landed this way, along with gun batteries, anti-tank guns and even more jeeps.

• About 70 million men fought in the war and about 55 million people may have died. These include 6 million Jews, one third of the Jews then living.

• During the Normandy landings in 1944, the Allies took their own harbour with them! A total of 64 blockships (codenamed GOOSEBERRIES) set sail with the invading forces to construct a breakwater, 213,000,000 tons of concrete and 70,000 tons of steel reinforcement for caissons, steel pontoon bridges and piers which adjusted to the tides (there was a difference of 23 feet (7 metres) between low and high tide). Called MULBERRY harbour, the American section was destroyed by the worst June storm in the Channel for 40 years, but the British artificial floating port was successfully floated to the landing spot and sunk into position. There it gave shelter to 500 ships and helped the troops to disembark at Arromanches.

Evacuees arriving at Eastbourne, Sussex, at the outbreak of war in 1939. In all, 827,000 schoolchildren were evacuated from major cities to seaside towns and rural areas in the autumn of that year, to escape from German bombing raids.

THE DIARY OF ANNE FRANK

For two years two Jewish families hid in a secret annexe above offices in Amsterdam, in constant fear of discovery and not daring to come out. This is described vividly in *The Diary of Anne Frank*; its young author was only 13 when she began the diary. She tells of the claustrophobic conditions and how sometimes the family could not wash or go to the toilet for fear the sound might be heard from below. Food was smuggled up to them by friends who had once worked with Mr Frank. The rest of the staff in the offices below had no idea these rooms existed.

Anne was captured in August 1944, along with the other seven occupants of the annexe, when German Gestapo suddenly arrived in the building and demanded that the secret door, hidden behind a hinged bookcase, be opened. They had been betrayed. Anne and her sister died in the concentration camp at Belsen and only her father - and the diary - survived.

LEFT: *A mushroom cloud, trademark of the atomic bomb, rises over Hiroshima on 6th August 1945.*
RIGHT: *Picture of Anne Frank taken from her famous diary*
BELOW: *Allied troops landing on the beaches of Normandy on D-Day (Decisive Day), 6th June 1944.*

THE AMERICAS

1974 Watergate. President Nixon, a Republican, is forced to resign after a political scandal. An attempt to bug the offices of his opponents in the Watergate building is discovered.

1974 Portugal A military coup restores democracy and ends the colonial war.

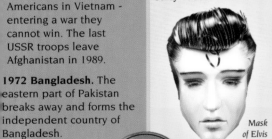

1974 Cyprus. Turkish troops invade northern Cyprus, in response to a coup backed by the colonels who rule Greece to overthrow the moderate president Archbishop Makarios, by militants who want 'enosis', the union of Greece with Cyprus. Turkish troops invade and occupy 35 percent of the Greek island, with the aim of protecting the Turkish Cypriot minority. Many thousands of Greek Cypriots become refugees. The ruling military dictatorship of Greece collapses four days later and democracy is restored. The Turkish occupation goes on to cause tension in the area for years to come.

1979 USSR Invades Afghanistan, on the request of the pro-Soviet ruler, to stop a civil war and protect Soviet interests. This invasion is seen as the same mistake as that made by the Americans in Vietnam - entering a war they cannot win. The last USSR troops leave Afghanistan in 1989.

1972 Bangladesh. The eastern part of Pakistan breaks away and forms the independent country of Bangladesh.

1970s Silicon Chip is invented in the United States and it revolutionizes the electronics industry.

1972 In Kenya scientists discover a skull 2.5 million years old, belonging to an early ancestor of human beings.

1972 The American, Mark Spitz, is the first person to win seven gold medals at a single Olympic Games.

1977 Astronomers see rings around Uranus for the first time.

1978 The world's first "test-tube baby is born in Britain. Baby Louise's birth is a result of the pioneering research of Patrick Steptoe and Dr Robert Edwards.

1979 Nicaragua. The Sandinita government comes to power after the overthrow of President Somoza and remains in control until 1990.

1975 Spain's Chief of State, General Franco, dies. Juan Carlos, grandson of the last King of Spain, becomes the first King of Spain in 41 years.

1978 Karol Wojtyla, a Polish cardinal, becomes the first non-Italian pope for 400 years. He has taken the name John Paul II. He survives an assassination attempt in 1981, while blessing the crowd in St. Peter's Square.

1979 Margaret Thatcher is elected first woman Prime Minister of Britain.

1979 Iran. A revolution forces the Shah to leave and religious leader, Ayatollah Khomeini, becomes ruler of a new Muslim republic.

1977 Tenerife Air Crash. The world's worst-ever aviation disaster kills 504 passengers when an American Pan Am and a Dutch KLM jumbo jet collide on the ground at Tenerife airport in the Canary Islands. 70 Pan Am passengers survive the crash.

1976 China. Mao Tse-Tung, the Chinese communist leader, dies at the age of 82.

1977 Elvis Presley, the king of rock'n'roll, who dies at the age of 42, dominated pop music in the late 1950s and early 1960s.

Mask of Elvis

1979 Compact Disc. The Dutch company Philips and the Japanese company Sony co-develop the compact disc.

1976 The Concorde, the first passenger plane to fly faster than sound begins flights across the Atlantic.

1980 John Lennon, the former Beatle, is shot dead in New York. His killer, Mark Chapman, has no obvious motive but his obsession for Lennon.

c.1980 Personal Stereos goe on sale. Now people can listen to music without disturbing others.

1981 'Columbia' is the first space shuttle to orbit the earth. Unlike rockets, it can take off into space and land again many times.

1982 Falkland Islands. Argentina invades British owned Falkland Islands. Britain regains control by sending a task force.

Solidarñosc

1980 Poland. The Solidarity trade union, led by Lech Walesa, demands better working conditions for workers. The government brings in martial law.

1989 The Berlin Wall is torn down. (See key feature on page 39)

1985 The USSR. Mikhail Gorbachev becomes leader. He begins a new age of 'Glasnost' and 'Perestroika' (openness and rebuilding).

1986 The USSR. A disaster at the Chernobyl nuclear power plant causes widespread radioactive pollution.

1989-1990 Popular Protests lead to the end of total communist control, and free elections in Poland, Hungary, East Germany, Czechoslovakia and Romania.

1980 The Iran~Iraq War. Border conflict develops into a full-scale war. Iraq's objective is to gain control of the Statt-al-Arab waterway, which has been under joint Iraqi-Iranian control since 1975. The war ends in 1988.

1980 Zimbabwe. Robert Mugabe becomes the Prime Minister of the independent African republic of Zimbabwe, (formerly Rhodesia.). Armed resistance by black African groups and an international economic boycott, force Prime Minister Ian Smith to allow democratic elections in the country he declared independent from British rule in 1965.

1984-1990 African Famine After years without rain Ethiopia, Sudan and Chad suffer terrible famine. Thousands die from starvation and disease.

1982 Aids virus. Scientists at the Pasteur Institute in France and at the US National Cancer Institute discover the micro-organism (virus) that causes AIDS, or Acquired Immune Deficiency Syndrome, which damages the immune system and leave sufferers unable to resist infectious diseases.

1980s-1990s Fight Against Drugs. The US Government spends increasing sums of money to prevent the violence and suffering caused by trade in illegal drugs.

1985 Much of Mexico City is destroyed by a huge earthquake which kills 5,000 and leaves many homeless.

1985 Columbia's Nevado del Ruiz volcano erupts, killing 25,000 people, and buries the town of Armero under a blanket of burning mud.

1982-1983 Nuclear Weapons Protest. Many thousands of people attend protest rallies all over Europe and the USA. They oppose nuclear arms as well as nuclear energy, and are part of the ecological or 'green' movement.

1985 India. In the world's worst industrial disaster over 2000 die from gas poisoning at Bhopal.

1986 Philippines. Dictator Ferdinand Marcos is deposed.

1985 'Live Aid' concerts, telecast worldwide, raise over £40 million for victims of African drought.

1986 The Russian Mir Space Station is launched.

1987 Channel Tunnel. Work begins to link Britain and France. 'The Chunnel' opens in May 1994.

1988 Barbara Harris is elected the first woman bishop in American Episcopal Church. Many Churches continue to argue about whether women can be priests.

1992 Bill Clinton, 42nd US President, becomes the first Democrat leader since Jimmy Carter was defeated by Ronald Reagan in 1980. He wins his 2nd term in The White House in 1996. In 1998 and 1999 allegations about his private life shake his presidency, but he remains a popular president.

1985 Much of Mexico City is Destroyed by a huge earthquake which kills 5,000 and leaves many homeless.

1990 The USSR. The republics of Lithuania and Estonia demand independence from the rest of the USSR.

1990 Lech Walesa becomes the first freely elected president of Poland for 50 years. The trade union Solidarity was made legal in 1989

1991 End of Communist Rule (See key feature on page 39).

1993 Peace Treaty between Israeli Prime Minister Itzhak Rabin and Yasser Arafat, Chairman of the PLO, is signed in the presence of President Clinton. The agreement provides a limited Palestinian autonomy in the Gaza strip and the West Bank.

1990-1991 Gulf Crisis Iraqi troops invade Kuwait in 1990, leading to 'Desert Storm', the war waged by the multi-national force against Saddam Hussein in January 1991. By February Saddam withdraws.

1990 Nelson Mandela is released from prison. He is a symbol of hope for those agaist apartheid. In 1994 he becomes South Africa's first black president.

1980s-1990s Ecology Movements. Fear that human activity may be destroying the natural world lead people to question our rapid industrial development. Pollution is a major problem and world governments express concern about the 'greenhouse effect' which many scientists believe is changing the earth's climate.

1994 Major Earthquake shakes Los Angeles killing 34 people and causes havoc throughout the city.

1994 IRA announces ceasefire to open the way for political settlement in Northern Ireland. In 1996 the cease-fire collapses.

1996 Dunblane. In the Scotish town of Dunblane, Thomas Hamilton, a former youth leader, walks into the school gymnasium and shoots dead 16 five and six year old children and one of their teachers. He then shoots himself.

and it emerged as a political party. Lech Walesa, its leader, wins the 1990 presidential elections and brings the struggle against the communist government to an end.

ASIA

1995 Nuclear Testing. France carries out it's fifth underground nuclear test at Mururoa Atoll in the South Pacific Ocean. many countries protest and demand an immediate ban on nuclear testing.

1996 Dolly the sheep is the first animal to be cloned. (See key feature on page 40).

1996 Life on Mars. NASA scientists believe fossil evidence of life on Mars is found inside a meteorite. A mission to bring back further samples for analysis is planned for 2000.

1997 Land Speed Record. The British jet-powered car Thrust SSC, becomes the first land vehicle to break the sound barrier. (See picture on page 39).

1997 Princess Diana (See key feature on page 3

1997 The Town of Ass is struck by a powerful earthquake which damages the famou 13th century Basili of Saint Francis, killing 11 people and makes 5000 people homeless

1997 Hong Kong a British colony since 1842 is handed back to the people of China. The new arrangement of governing the region is 'one country, two systems', where the communist system of China will coexist with the democratic system of Hong Kong.

1997 China. Deng Xiaoping, the Chinese leader, dies at the age of 92. Most people remember him for his strong beliefs in safeguarding the established order. Others remember him for his wide-ranging economic reforms whi led to China becoming one of the fastest-growing economies in the world. His success is Jiang Zemin.

1997 In Egypt, Muslin fanatics who belong to militant group called Gamoa, kill 58 tourists men, women and children, visiting the famous Temple of Hatshepsut. One of th leaders is in prison fo assassinating the Presid of Egypt, Anwar Sadat, 1981. This group is bit over the peace treaty v Israel and is against th government for not be strict in the practice o the laws of Islam.

1997 Mother Teresa of Calcutta, dies at the age of 87. The Nobel peace prize-winning Catholic missionary dedicated her life to helping the poor in India. She founded the Order o Missionaries of Charity in 1950 which now has 500 charity houses in more than 100 countries. Mothe Teresa was born Agn Gonxha Bojaxhiu in Skopje, Albania, whi is now Macedonia.

1996 Mini discs are launched in Japan.

Omagh Car kills 26 and more than 200 Carnival day. This worst single [day] during the 30 [years] of troubles in [Northe]rn Ireland. The [...] is the work of a [break]away IRA group [who ca]ll themselves [Real IRA'] and who [...] the Good [...] peace deal.

1999 The Euro. On January 1, 1999, a single currency , the euro, is launched in 11 countries of the European community. This marks the start of the European economic and monetary union, known as EMU.
1999 Berlin becomes once again the capital of the reunited Germany and the restored Reichstag its new seat of government.

Northern Ireland Peace Deal. The Irish [nation]alists, who believe that the British province of [Norther]n Ireland should be part of a [...] Ireland, and the Unionists who [... to] keep the link with Britain, enter [negoti]ations with the British and the Irish [govern]ments in search for peace in the province. A historic settlement is [reache]d on Good Friday to end three [decad]es of bloodshed, by creating an all-party [assemb]ly, a framework for illegal arms to be handed [...] the release of political prisoners.

Northern Ireland
Mainland Britain

[G]ermany's Worst Railway Disaster since the [Secon]d World War, kills 101 people and injures 80, [as a] high-speed train fractures a wheel and [crashe]s onto a concrete bridge near Hanover.

1999 In Kosovo, ethnic Albanians outnumber [Serb]s, by nine to one. The Kosovo Liberation Army [for] Albanian rights and the land which both sides [claim] to be historically theirs. During the hostilities [peop]le, mostly Albanians. The two sides eventually [... t]o negotiate and consider the international [...]plan, which gives [Ko]sovo Albanians [autono]my, that is the [...] self-government, [...]independence, [Int]ernational peace [...]rejected by the [Serbian] President [Serbi]an Milosevic. [Th]en NATO countries [... ou]t air strikes on [Serbia] to stop its ethnic [cleansi]ng. The Serbs [... a]gree to withdraw [tro]ops from Kosovo [...]the return of the [refug]ee/Albanian refugees.

1999 King Hussein of Jordan, the moderate monarch, who played a major role in the Middle East peace process, dies at the age of 63. He became king at the age of 17 in 1953. His reign was dominated by the territorial struggle between Arabs and Jews. His diplomatic efforts during the Middle East peace talks have earned him the respect of many world leaders.

[A]irstrikes on [Iraq b]egin in a joint [Americ]an and British [opera]tion code-named [Desert] Fox. This came [...] after reports that [Sadda]m persistently [refuse]d to let United [Nation]s weapon [inspec]tors visit sites [and ga]in access to [docume]nts regarding [his] weapons of mass [destru]ction.

1990. The Hubble Space Telescope is launched in the USA (*see inside back cover*).
1999 - 2000 The Millennium Bug. There is speculation that computers might fail to recognize the '00' of the year 2000, resulting in computer breakdowns and consequently causing great disruption around the world.

[...] US Embassies [bomb]ed in Nairobi, [...] and Tanzania by [Islami]c extremists, [killing] over 200 people [and inj]uring thousands. [There]after, US cruise [missil]es struck targets in [...]against those the [Americ]ans believed to be [respon]sible for the blasts.

[G]lobal Storms cause havoc in many countries, [among] them the USA, Britain, Kenya and Bangladesh. [The we]ather phenomenon El Nino, causes severe [floodin]g in Peru and Bolivia. In Honduras, [Hurrican]e Mitch claims 11000 lives and devastates [most o]f the country. It will take many years to [reconst]ruct the country and restore its economy.

[D]VD Technology [and Di]gital TV. (*See key [feature o]n page 40*)

1948-2000 The Computer Age. (*See key feature on page 40*)

[2000] A New Millennium. [Mank]ind is celebrating the dawn of a new [mille]nnium. This event has become the focus [for ou]r hopes and resolutions, for it holds [the pr]omise of a better future.

AD1970 TO AD2000 ~ A NEW MILLENIUM

THE EUROPEAN UNION

The Euro

In 1957 six European nations signed the Treaty of Rome, setting up the European Economic Community, or Common Market. It aims to free the movement of workers, goods and money between the member states. Over the next 40 years, the "six" were joined by several other countries (*see chart*). These 15 states are now known as the European Community, whose 340 million people provide a market larger than the USA or Japan.

A single currency, the euro, was introduced in 1999. Some European politicians see the euro as a necessary and significant step towards full political union.

The six founding nations

Belgium	 1957
France	 1957
Germany	 1957
Italy	 1957
Luxembourg	. . 1957
Netherlands	. . . 1957

Date of entry of the other nine nations

Denmark	 1973
Ireland	 1973
United Kingdom	. . . 1973
Greece	 1981
Portugal	 1986
Spain	 1986
Sweden	 1995
Finland	 1995
Austria	 1995

PRINCESS DIANA

In 1997, Diana Princess of Wales, died at the age of 36 after the car in which she was travelling crashed at high speed in a tunnel in Paris. Dodi Fayed, her friend, and the car's driver, also died in the crash.

Britain went into mourning. Grieving crowds gathered for many days outside the gates of Kensington Palace, in London to pay their respects, creating a vast mountain of flower tributes. Diana succeeded in her wish to be "queen of people's hearts".

Prince Charles and Princess Diana divorced in 1996. She remained a member of the British royal family and shared responsibility for their sons William and Harry. She will be remembered as a warm human being who campaigned for many causes, including the welfare of children, the plight of AIDS sufferers, and the abolition of landmines around the world.

She was in life, as well as in death, an icon.

Princess Diana in Korea

1989 THE BERLIN WALL IS TORN DOWN

The wall was built in 1961 to stop refugees from communist East Berlin, crossing the border into West Germany. But since Gorbachev's reforms encouraged democratic movements across Eastern Europe, communist regimes gradually lost power. The East German government, realizing that reforms were needed to pacify public unrest, declared that East Germans were free to leave the country at any point along the border, including the Berlin wall crossing points. That same night, 10th November , jubilant German crowds from East and West, gathered by the wall to celebrate the end of this symbol of repression.

In 1990 Germany is reunited, 45 years after the end of the Second World War.

1991 END OF COMMUNISM IN THE USSR

Hardline Communists, on 19th August 1991, mounted a coup and toppled President Gorbachev. To enforce their authority they banned demonstrations and put tanks on the streets of Moscow. The resistance, led by Boris Yeltsin, President of the Russian Republic, rallied in support of Gorbachev and urged the soldiers to mutiny and the workers to strike. Thousands of people and many army officers supported him. The coup collapsed and the troops were ordered to withdraw from Moscow. Gorbachev was reinstated, but was now powerless without the support of the Soviet Communist Party which was now disgraced.

On 21st December 1991, the Commonwealth of Independent States (CIS) was founded by Russia, Ukraine and Byelorussia, and joined by eight other Soviet republics who opted for independence soon after the coup collapsed. Mikhail Gorbachev, the Soviet executive President, resigned on 25th December, because the Soviet Union had disintegrated.

Mikhail Gorbachev

1997 Land-speed record. The British jet car, Thrust SSC in the Nevada desert, driven by Andy Green, who becomes the first man to break the sound barrier on land, with acceleration figures of 0.760 mph in 27 seconds.

A pilot training in a Virtual Reality environment.

THE COMPUTER AGE 1948 - 2000

The Manchester Mark I, the first electronic computer to store and process information, is made in Britain in 1948. All computers work on the binary system. That means the processor in the computer reads and converts all the information into two digits, 0s and 1s. Now, computers are part of everyday life, worldwide, and have become a major source of information and recreation in the workplace and at home. It is without doubt one of the most important technological achievements of the 20th century.

One of the recent developments is **IBM's Via Voice**, which turns continuous speech into accurate written words on the computer screen.

1980s-1990s Virtual Reality technology allows you to interact with computer generated worlds, from flight simulators training new pilots to role-playing arcade games.

1980s-1990s The Internet. The worldwide computer network is creating a new borderless world for people to interact in business and personal matters.

Special Effects in the Movies. Computer-generated special effects create amazing and realistic dinosaurs in *Jurassic Park*, a lovable dragon in *Dragonheart*, and brought to life the tragic story of the sinking of the *Titanic*, in the most commercially successful movie to date, *Titanic*. *Terminator 2*, *The Fifth Element* and *Star Wars* are among the movies which used computer special effects to their advantage.

Computer Games have improved beyond recognition since the first game was released in 1972, in which a player intercepted a moving 'dot'. In recent computer games the player interacts with flight simulators, driving games, war games, sports games and adventure games.

1990s Digital Television. Digital technology, which records and transmits picture and sound information as a series of numbers, '0's and '1's, just like the code used in computers (a 'byte'), is now revolutionizing the quality of television viewing in our homes. Sound and pictures are as good as the original source.

1990s Digital Video Disc (DVD). The digital technology, already used in music CDs, is now employed in the Digital Video Discs, which not only store digital sound, but also digital pictures. This is ideal for movies, concerts and other activities where vision and sound are equally important.

The digital video disc (DVD) stores information in two layers. The lazer beam reads both layers at the same time.

1998 The First Digital Radios are on sale. The sound quality of digital radio broadcasting is almost as good as a Compact Disc (CD). Interference caused by the weather and by the obstruction of high buildings has come to an end.

GENETICS

Genetics is the study of heredity - the handing down of characteristics of living things from one generation to another. Genetics, as a science, began over 100 years ago with Gregor Mendel, whose experiments with cross-breeding sweet peas showed that 'particles', now called genes, are responsible for passing characteristics from parents to offspring. In 1953, the American biologist James Watson and the English biochemist Francs Crick worked out the structure of DNA, which contains the genetic information for reproduction in every living cell.

Making a list of the three billion different "letters" in human DNA will lead to identifying the genes responsible for hereditary diseases and gene therapy may be possible.

Genetic Engineering. By the 1970s biochemists were able to alter the genetic structure of plants to produce new varieties of crop with, for instance, greater resistance to diseases. Furthermore, gene technology provided food with altered characteristics, such as seedless grapes, bigger potatoes and tomatoes with longer shelf-life. The lack of research and information available about the growing number of genetically modified (GM) foods, worried some consumer and environmental groups, and they demanded more testing to find out if the new food is suitable for human consumption.

Cloning. A clone is a living creature copied from genetic material taken from a single individual. In Scotland in 1996, the scientist Ian Wilmut successfully cloned a sheep, named Dolly, out of a single cell from another sheep's udder. The future medical applications of this science are seen by some to be beneficial to infertile couples, and as a way of making organs for transplantation or saving endangered species. Cloning also causes anxieties, one of the most important issues being the possibility of cloning a human being, and the consequences of this.

Dolly the sheep. The first animal to be cloned.

THE 20TH-CENTURY SKYSCRAPER

In the second half of the 19th century, advanced technology made the building of large-scale structures possible. Paxton's Crystal Palace in Hyde Park, London, built to house the Great Exhibition of 1851, with its gigantic iron frame, filled in with sheets of glass, showed the way forward to a new style of building, practical and functional. The metal structure of Eiffel Tower in Paris (1889), is another striking example of architectural engineering.

Further technological advances, such as the development of reinforced concrete (concrete strengthened on the inside by steel bars, tied together), the availability of strong plates of glass and the invention of the high-speed lift in the 1870s, led to the construction of the skyscraper. The metal framework was now capable of carrying the entire weight of a high structure. The world's first skyscraper is the Home Insurance Building (1883-85) in Chicago, which is 10 storeys high.

Prosperous businesses saw the skyscraper as the ultimate symbol of success, and added even more storeys to their new buildings. In New York, in 1930, the Chrysler Building reached 77 storeys and 1047 feet (319 meters) high. A year later, the Empire State Building reached 102 storeys and 1250 feet (380 meters) high, dominating ever since the skyline of Manhattan, New York.

Other cities and towns in the United States, Europe, Africa and Asia followed New York's example and began to build skyscrapers. Their skylines reflected the new architectural styles and they began to develop into spectacular modern cities.

The world's tallest building is under construction. It is the Shanghai World Financial Centre, in China, and is due for completion in 2001. The skyscraper will be 1509 feet (460m) tall - higher than the Sears Tower in Chicago, which is 1453 feet (443m) high. Even now, in Japan, plans are under way for an even taller building.

The Empire State Building, New York.

SPACE ~ THE FINAL FRONTIER

THE FIRST MEN ON THE MOON

July 20 1969 was one of the most exciting days in the history of exploration for it was then that the first men stepped on to land that was not of this earth. Neil Armstrong, commander of Apollo II, stepping off the ladder of the lunar module, marked this dramatic event with the words, 'That's one small step for man, one giant leap for mankind.' Soon he was joined by Edwin 'Buzz' Aldrin while Michael Collins, a third astronaut, remained in orbit around the moon in the main Apollo II spacecraft.' The surface is fine and powdery,' Neil Armstrong remarked. 'It's different, but it's very pretty out here.' Bouncing slowly over the surface, testing out the effects of moving in such low gravity, the two astronauts planted the American 'Stars and Stripes' flag, took photographs and collected samples of dust and rock for scientists back on Earth to examine.

SPACE PROBES

Unmanned space probes now send pictures back from planets that are hundreds of millions of miles away. The most notable are the Voyager I and Voyager 2 space probes, which embarked, in the late 1970's, on a 12-year journey to explore Jupiter, Saturn, Uranus, Neptune and other planets and their moons. When the Voyagers beamed their pictures to Earth, the images on view surpassed all expectations.

SPACE STATIONS

SKYLAB. The first US space station, Skylab, was partially constructed from recycled components from the Apollo Moon missions. Between 1973 and 1974, nine astronauts lived on Skylab and carried out many experiments. **MIR.** The Russian space station Mir was launched in 1986 and it remained manned for over thirteen years. The Russian Valeri Poliakov, spent a record 438 days on the space station. Mir has had a troubled history, but the knowledge gained on how zero gravity affects the human body, is invaluable.

INTERNATIONAL SPACE STATION (ISS) Many countries around the world are cooperating to built the world's largest space station. The first part was launched in 1998 and it will take at least 6 years to complete.

Saturn 5 *rocket launches all Apollo craft*   *Edwin Aldrin on the Moon*   Space Shuttle Discovery *lifts off*

Footprint on the Moon   *The Apollo 11 crew: Neil Armstrong, Michael Collins and Edwin Aldrin*

SPACE EVENTS AND MISSIONS OF THE 20TH CENTURY

1926   Launch of first liquid fuel rocket.
1957   Launch of Soviet Sputnik I, the world's first artificial satellite.
1957   Soviet dog Laika, becomes first living creature in space.
1959   US Vanguard 2, takes first photograph of Earth.
1959   Soviet Luna 3, takes first photograph of the hidden side of the Moon.
1961   Soviet Venera I, makes flyby of Venus.
1961   Soviet Yuri Gagarin, becomes the first cosmonaut to orbit the Earth in Vostok I.
1961   Alan Shepard becomes first US astronaut to fly in space.
1962   John Glenn becomes first astronaut to orbit the Earth.
1963   Soviet Valentina Tereshkova is the first woman in space in Vostok 6.
1964   First flyby of Mars made by US Mariner 4.
1964   First close-up pictures of the Moon's surface by US Ranger 7.
1965   First space walk by Soviet cosmonaut Alexei Leonov.
1966   Soviet Luna 9 becomes first craft to land on the Moon.
1967   Three astronauts die in a fire on the launch pad of Apollo I.
1968   The first humans orbit the Moon in US Apollo 8.

1969   US astronaut Neil Armstrong becomes the first person to walk on the Moon.
1970   Soviet Venera 7 is the first probe to land on Venus.
1970   Soviet Lunokhod I becomes the first rover to drive on the Moon.
1971   Launch of Soviet Salyut I, the world's first space station.
1973   The first US space station, Skylab, is launched.
1973   US Mariner 10 takes first detailed picture of Mercury.
1975   First time a US and Soviet spacecraft, Apollo-Soyuz, dock together.
1975   Soviet Venera 9 takes first picture of the surface of the planet Venus.
1976   US probe Viking I becomes first craft to land successfully on Mars.
1977   US Voyager I and Voyager 2 send the first images of Jupiter, Saturn, Uranus and Neptune.
1978   First international space observatory is set up by UK, USA and European Space Agency.
1979   US Pioneer 11 discovers a new moon and ring for Saturn.
1980   US Voyager I discovers six additional moons for Saturn.
1981   Launch of the first reusable US space shuttle, Columbia.
1984   US astronaut Bruce McCandless uses the Manned Manoeuvering Unit to move independently outside the spacecraft.